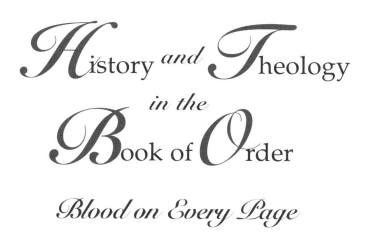

History and Theology
in the
Book of Order

Blood on Every Page

with
Leader's Guide

D1607092

William E. Chapman

Witherspoon Press
Louisville, Kentucky

Edited by Cassandra D. Williams

Book interior and cover design by Peg Coots Alexander

Cover Photo: Makemie's Trial. Courtesy of Presbyterian Historical Society, Philadelphia, Pennsylvania.

First edition

Published by Witherspoon Press, a Ministry of the General Assembly Council, Congregational Ministries Division, Presbyterian Church (U.S.A.), Louisville, Kentucky

Web site address: www.pcusa.org/witherspoonpress

PRINTED IN THE UNITED STATES OF AMERICA

06 07 08 09 10 11 12 13 14 15 — 10 9 8 7 6 5 4 3 2

Library of Congress Cataloging-in-Publication Data
Chapman, William E.
    History and theology in the Book of order : blood on every page : leader's guide / William E. Chapman. — 1st ed.
      p.   cm.
    Includes bibliographical references and index.
    ISBN 1-57153-016-9
    1. Presbyterian Church (U.S.A.) Book of order. 2. Presbyterian Church (U.S.A.) — Government. I. Title.
BX8969.6.P743C48 1999
262'. 05137—dc21
                                      99-21216

To those who drafted the
Historic Principles of Church Order
and to those who will continue to carry them
into the twenty-first century.

Contents

Acknowledgments

The seed from which this book grew was my discovery two years ago of an 1834 copy of The Constitution of the Presbyterian Church in the United States of America in The Owl Pen, a second-hand bookstore northeast of Albany, New York. I considered the $10 price to be a bargain. My excitement at this instance of Providence surprised those who had accompanied me on the expedition. When I examined the book, I was surprised to find Scripture references for the Form of Government, as well as the Westminster Confession and Catechisms. Apparently, Presbyterians nearly two centuries ago understood their government to have been built on the foundation of Scripture and the Westminster Confession. To consider the *Book of Order* as the fruit of reflection on these two foundations as they sought to be faithful in their life together was the insight behind this work.

My bookstore discovery fed a long-held interest in polity. One of my hobbies is reading about the United States Supreme Court. This hobby began in 1963, when the church I was serving in Wisconsin struggled with the Civil Rights Act and its impact on our country. I decided that I needed to learn more about the "third branch" of our government, so I began reading whatever I could find in this area. At the time, the Supreme Court was talked about without much knowledge, and I wanted to understand this branch of government better. The hobby continues.

My interest in polity was further heightened when I served on the Presbyteries' Cooperative Committee on Examinations for Candidates. Administering the "ords" offered an important perspective on how Presbyterians across our denomination find in our polity many ways of being Presbyterian while working from the same text. I was also privileged to watch persons dedicated to our polity wrestle with the issues of how to design examinations appropriate for entry-level knowledge of polity. For this "graduate-level" exposure to life in our church, I continue to be deeply grateful.

When I decided to leave that position in 1991, I noticed that the polity professor at Princeton was retiring. I wrote Princeton offering to substitute in the position until a permanent faculty person was recruited. As of this writing, I am still an adjunct.

Teaching polity to Presbyterian students at both Princeton Theological Seminary and New Brunswick Seminary has been an exciting venture. What began as a temporary adjunct assignment at Princeton in 1992 has become a continuing adventure, with the stimulation that comes uniquely when seminarians wrestle with the way we Presbyterians go about being the church. They have enriched my understanding and informed my awareness of implications I could never have imagined alone. They have also sharpened my concern as they revealed how urgent it is to train newly elected officers for their responsibilities. My concern grew as many who had served on sessions told me, "I wish I had known that when I served on session." The stories that followed this all too frequent introduction were enough to make one weep.

A providential find in a bookstore, a long-standing hobby, together with ongoing contact with seminarians all contributed to this project, but the specific trigger was a conversation with my good friend Clifford Sherrod. At lunch one day as I was talking about the class in polity I was teaching, he asked, "Why don't you quit talking and write a book about it?" His candor and directness started this project. I am most appreciative of his encouragement, which included serving as a second reader as the book progressed.

Throughout this period, my wife Zitta has been a continuing supporter and encourager. She was certain I would produce a book long before I thought it possible. Her initial reading of the manuscript, and her suggestions offered lovingly have stirred me to do more than I thought possible. I continue to count our marriage as a demonstration of God's gracious love, for which I continually give thanks.

I accept responsibility for those errors that testify to human limitations. I hope that these will not unduly restrict the discussion I anticipate as a result of this effort. Indeed, it is my wish that this book will open up a fresh avenue of discussion of how it is we Presbyterians understand our effort to be the body of Christ in today's world. In the spirit of conversation, I look forward to continuing the discussion via e-mail at william.chapman@pcusa.org or polywonk@aol.com.

I am deeply grateful to the staff of Witherspoon Press whose commitment and counsel in this project have been most helpful. Beth Basham convinced me that this project was worth doing. Casey Williams shepherded me through the publication maze with clarity and good humor. It has been genuinely pleasant to work as part of such a cooperative team. They have demonstrated the spirit of mutual support and admonition that is appropriate for those of us who seek together to glorify our God and our Savior.

*I*ntroduction

*T*he subtitle of this book, *Blood on Every Page,* is drawn from a conversation with a Presbyterian elder. Like many, he had "married into the Presbyterian church" after being raised as a Roman Catholic, and was eventually elected an elder. Without any training or much awareness of what lay behind them, he assented to some vows when he was ordained. They sounded important, so he responded appropriately when the time came.

He was subsequently appointed elder to the personnel committee by the moderator. During his time of service on this committee, a conflict erupted on the pastoral staff. The elder found himself caught between two persons whom he considered friends. His distress was intensified by the volume and diversity of advice he received from members of the congregation. In response to the staff crisis, the elder decided to read the *Book of Order,* which he had received earlier. He approached it as people often approach the Bible during a crisis. He took his *Book of Order* with him on vacation, where he had time to read it from beginning to end!

The elder and I spoke at a social affair shortly after he finished this marathon reading. He initiated the conversation by asking whether I was still teaching polity at a Presbyterian seminary. When I said that I was, he got very serious and then gravely said, "Tell your students that our *Book of Order* has blood on every page." Since then, I have used his phrase frequently. Of course there isn't any actual blood on any page. However, this elder, in the middle of a difficult time for the church and for himself, discerned that the *Book of Order* contains evidence that church people had resolved painful conflicts in the past and had discovered better, wiser ways of approaching certain recurring tasks in the life of the church. His comment reflects a discerning eye that was able to appreciate the inherited wisdom found in the *Book of Order.*

Another discerning eye belonged to a sociologist of religion, Paul Harrison, whose description of church polity is more analytical.

Polity is the sociological manifestation of doctrinal belief; it is the political expression of the content of the gospel as interpreted by members of the religious group. However, polity, because it has other functions, is never the perfect expression of religious belief. Even a system of doctrine is never consistent in all respects. One of the most effective ways of discovering internal contradictions within a doctrinal system is to study the dilemmas experienced by the church when its people attempt to express their beliefs through their polity.[1]

Harrison describes, in sociological terms, the underlying dynamics of church polity. He calls attention to the dialectic between faith and order, noting that the correspondence between the two is never absolute.

Far from being chiseled in stone, every edition of the *Book of Order* prominently displays a time span during which that edition is valid. The dynamic noted by Harrison is thus validated in a small, yet strong way. Presbyterians spell out how the *Book of Order* is changed in G-18.0300. Changes, or amendments, are now printed in bold type the year after they are adopted. An index appears at the beginning of the *Book of Order* that lists where these changes can be found.

There is gentle humor in the fact that the hallmark of change in the *Book of Order* is printed in Latin—the only instance of Latin found in the *Book of Order*. The last line of G-2.0200 reads,

> The church affirms *Ecclesia reformata, semper reformanda*, that is, 'the church reformed, always reforming' according to the Word of God and the call of the Spirit.[2]

This study of Presbyterian Polity is a reminder that we, in the Reformed tradition, take history seriously, seeking to learn from the past as we face issues of faith in the present. It proposes an approach to understanding the *Book of Order* that recognizes this inherent dynamic of polity as a valuable guide.

In the first chapter of the *Book of Order* (not arranged chronologically as might be expected), are principles that have guided Presbyterians on their journey, and which still undergird the *Book of Order*. Footnotes to these principles reveal dates such as 1788, 1797, and 1910.[3] This material still appears as originally written, complete with complex, difficult to understand sentences and gender-specific pronouns. One very important, but too often overlooked, section of this chapter bears the title, "The Historic Principles of Church Order" (G-1.0300).

Echoing Harrison, the Report of the Special Committee on Historic Principles, Conscience, and Church Government to the 1983 General Assembly of the just reunited Presbyterian Church (U.S.A.) stated:

> The polity of Presbyterianism—with its strong insistence on the rule of the majority and the rights of the minority—is indeed the way in which Presbyterians affirm their unity amid their diversity. This polity not only organizes dissent and diversity, it is itself a product of dissent, diversity, compromise, and the creative resolution of bitter conflict.[4]

On May 23, 1785, the Synod of New York and Philadelphia created a committee of ten ministers whose stated objective was to take into consideration, the Constitution of the Church of Scotland, & other Protestant Churches; & agreeably to the general principles of Presbyterian Government, compile a system of general rules for the Government of the Synod, & the several Presbyteries under their inspection; & the People in their communion. & to make a report of their proceeding at the next meeting of Synod.[5]

The Synod finally voted "to ratify, & adopt the same, as now altered, & amended, as the Constitution of the Presbyterian Church in America"[6] on Wednesday, May 28, 1788. The Historic Principles were part of this vote. The following day, the synod divided itself into four synods and called the first meeting of the General Assembly for the following May.[7] This account validates the characterization by the 1983 Special Committee of the Polity of Presbyterianism as "a product of dissent, diversity, compromise, and the creative resolution of bitter conflict."[8]

The members of the committee were all ministers, including John Witherspoon who had signed the Declaration of Independence twelve years earlier. These pastors were living in a time when the writing and ratification of a Constitution for a new nation involved everyone. The guidance of the synod, through debate and amendment, was direct and vigorous. However, there was also a commitment to being Presbyterian and figuring out how to import that tradition into the new continent. Through it all, the commitment of synod was to building up the body of Christ.

My first exposure to the Historic Principles was in the mid-seventies when I first became a reader at a reading group for grading the ordination examinations administered by Presbyteries' Cooperative Committee on Examinations for Candidates. The Examination in Church Polity included a required question on the Historic Principles. The person explaining the question and the response told us that the reason such material was included was to ensure that each candidate understood the Presbyterian ethos. No clarification was given as to why this was so. The impression I gained was that the principles were Presbyterian roots and were important simply because they were roots.

The purpose of this book is to provide an approach to the Historic Principles that provides insight about the Presbyterian ethos. The Historic Principles provide the framework for exploration. Each principle identifies a tension that is present in the life of Christian community and in so doing provides cautions for us as we go about our mission. These tensions could be called paradoxes, polarities, or even dilemmas. Whatever they are called, they are a fact of life in any religious community. By identifying them, the Historic Principles serve to provide "way-points" as we seek to be faithful disciples.

In order to understand the Historic Principles, we need to use a careful method of interpretation. Our guide for interpretation will be G-1.0500, where the Constitution of the Presbyterian Church (U.S.A.) is defined as the *Book of Confessions*, and the *Book of Order*. The process will be to explore the interplay between Scripture, the *Book of Confessions*, and the *Book of Order*.[9] This might be called a "constitutional approach to Presbyterian polity." I have discovered as I followed this approach that the *Book of Order* has as its theme "Caring for the Body of Christ." The places where the *Book of Order* is prescriptive are those places where the risk of harming brother and sister Presbyterian members of the body of Christ is high. Often the *Book of Order* appears to restrict choices when, in fact, the danger is more theological than about lack of compliance to a specific provision. The type of caring presented in the *Book of Order* is neither mushy nor emotional. There is a realism that illuminates the dark and difficult spaces of life together. The Historic Principles make it clear that the body of Christ has boundaries in as much as it is a human institution. To move beyond those limits is to live with a continuing challenge to "the ways things currently are." However, Presbyterians tend to resist proposals for major shifts in doctrine or in order. Change occurs with deliberate speed.

I, in fact, discovered a disciplined spirituality as I worked on this project. Our Presbyterian polity may be approached from various perspectives. Some ask, "What does the *Book of Order* say we have to do about . . .?" Others wonder, "What can't I do that I want to?" Still others ponder, "What are we (am I) supposed to be doing?" All these questions presuppose the sort of answer that will be found in study of the *Book of Order*. Perhaps the most challenging part of living with our polity lies in finding new ways of asking ourselves what it means to live in a community of disciples.

The challenge is how we can be good stewards of our heritage. In all the discussions about how much and in which direction the *Book of Order* should be amended or recast, there is surprisingly little discussion of how the Historic Principles of chapter 1 might provide guidance for understanding this collection of wisdom, which is the product of several centuries of experience. The Historic Principles can provide a helpful framework as we prepare to chart our course as Presbyterian Christians in the twenty-first century, a framework for new modes of obedience as together we move forward in the mission we have been given by Jesus Christ.

Note to reader: This book is designed to be a living document, reflecting the dynamic nature of Presbyterian polity. Wide margins have been provided for ease of note taking. This space can also be used to note changes in polity from GA overtures.

otes

1. Paul M. Harrison, *Authority and Power in a Free Church Tradition* (Princeton, NJ: Princeton University Press, 1959), pp. 5–6. Harrison studied the American Baptist Convention, so his assessment is not limited to Presbyterian phenomena.

2. There is continuing discussion regarding how the Latin phrase should appear, as well as how it should be translated. William P. Thompson has suggested that since reformanda is a gerund, a more accurate translation would be, "the church reformed, but always being reformed." Whether this discussion will lead to amending this provision is yet to be decided. (Personal communication)

3. These are not the oldest materials found in the *Book of Order*. However, they are early materials for American Presbyterians.

4. "Historic Principles, Conscience, and Church Government" (Louisville: Office of the General Assembly, 1983), p. 1. Available from Presbyterian Distribution Service as OGA-88-059 for $4.00.

5. Guy S. Klett, ed., *Minutes of the Presbyterian Church in America: 1706–1788* (Philadelphia: Presbyterian Historical Society, 1976), p. 597. Capitalization and punctuation reflects the manuscripts transcribed in this volume.

6. Ibid., p. 636.

7. Ibid., p. 638.

8. "Historic Principles," p. l.

9. This approach is inherent in the ordination vows for ministers of the Word and Sacrament, elders, and deacons as outlined in G-14.0207 and G-14.0405b. The sequence of the vows, especially G-14.0207a–e and G-14.0405b(1)–(5) suggests that these are an integrated sequence, rather than separate and distinct vows without interrelation. The volume of information involved is intimidating, however, so the commitment housed within the vows is rarely fulfilled. The advent of the *Book of Confessions* on CD-ROM with word search capability (which has been used extensively in preparing this resource) makes it possible to fulfill G-14.0207c and G-14.0405b(3) (in particular, the last phrase, "will you be instructed and led by those confessions as you lead the people of God?"), with a facility undreamed of previously. We are now able to search out how a word or phrase has been used in our confessions, providing us with a bridge between Scripture texts and provisions in the *Book of Order*. This same word search ability with the *Book of Order* enables us to begin to grasp the import of this "library" and appreciate the nuances of meaning present in these resources.

1

First Things

The Title

"The Book"

*W*hat sort of book is the *Book of Order?* A response to this question reveals what the reader expects to find in the *Book of Order.* Care needs to be taken as the cover of this or any book is opened, since it is often the case that what is found is limited by what is expected.

As we begin this exploration, let us consider some "what ifs." What if the *Book of Order* were the following:

- a guide for "building up the body of Christ"?

- a "treasure in earthen vessels"?

- a challenge to deepen our discipleship and to witness to our faith in Jesus Christ?

- like the wisdom literature we find in the Bible?

What if the *Book of Order*

- offered counsel for effective ministry rather than disconnected commandments to be obeyed?

- resulted from careful exegesis of Scripture in concert with the *Book of Confessions*?

- reminded us of what it means to be Presbyterian Christians?

- presented a distinctive way to be the church?

- alerted us to the perils of being a community of faith?

- called us to move toward compliance?

Keep these "what ifs" in mind as we continue our exploration of the *Book of Order.*

"Of Order"

When encountering the word *order*, a reader may wonder which kind of order or whose order is presupposed, or may question which type of order is intended by the writer. How often we quickly decide that the reference is to alphabetical or chronological order or to an order of logical or priority, as if those were the only possibilities!

In the first chapter of Luke, the writer tells Theophilus that the account is set "in order." Which sort of order did the writer of Luke mean? Bible scholars still debate which type of order was intended. What if Luke were to reappear long enough to answer, "theological," would we then understand more about that Gospel?

Our Western tendency is to assume that "order" presupposes "linear." So when one reads, for example, Chinua Achebe's novel, *Things Fall Apart*, it may seem to lack sense, or to be going around in circles. Eventually, if the reader bears with the text, he/she finds that the order is not circular, but spiral.

Similarly, Mary Doria Russell's novels, *The Sparrow* and *The Children of God*, are complex in their organization, with chapters numbered in sequence, but dated in an uncommon fashion, similar to how stories are told in some traditions. Such a novel could be read chronologically by recording the dates on the chapter pages and reading them in chronological order, but this is contrary to the author's design.

The order intended in the *Book of Order* presupposes the beginning of Genesis where God, the Creator, brings order out of chaos. Order for the church is a response to God's gift of the church to us. It is not the only possible order, but it is an attempt to build on the foundation of Scripture and our confessions. There are numerous places where the order in the *Book of Order* appears not to make sense without an understanding of its theological underpinnings. In the endeavor to offer theological clarification, the importance of the *Book of Confessions* is revealed as a guide to understanding the *Book of Order*.

"Order" in the *Book of Order* is intended to be the expression of a faithful people honoring their Deliverer. There are lots of "shall's" in the *Book of Order* but no imperatives. The "shall's" depend on each person responsibly accepting the gift that comes through the experience of the church over the years. This order is a fragile one, dependent on the constancy of the community of faith. It is the order of the body of Christ, as we Presbyterians understand it.

Getting Started

The cover of the *Book of Order* clearly displays the years during which that edition is authoritative. The dates refer to the period between two meetings of the General Assembly, which usually take place in June. When the book is opened, the preface lists those amendments "declared made" (approved by a majority of the presbyteries) at the most recent General Assembly.[1] The text of new amendments is printed in bold type to alert readers to changes that have taken place since the previous edition. The number of amendments changes from year to year, sometimes dramatically.

The section following the preface, "Explanation of the Reference Number System of the *Book of Order*" guides the reader in finding specific provisions.

There are no page numbers in the *Book of Order*. The letter and decimal system provides more accuracy from year to year, and facilitates cross-reference between editions of the *Book of Order* in different languages. It takes some effort to learn how to find a reference to a specific provision, as it does to find chapter and verse in the Bible. Readers will discover, however, that it becomes easy once they stop looking for page numbers.

The contents of the *Book of Order* reveals that it is divided into three parts: "Form of Government"; "Directory for Worship"; and "Rules of Discipline." Within each part are several chapters that are, in turn, divided into major sections. The section headings are printed in bold type to indicate that they are summary statements and to avoid confusion of the headings with the text itself. Brief notes are found to the left of each paragraph that identify the subject of each paragraph, and serve as helps to the reader. These notes are not considered as authoritative as is the text.

The Most Important Chapter

Chapter 1 in "Form of Government " in the *Book of Order*, which is divided into five sections,[2] bears the title, "Preliminary Principles." This has been the title of the first chapter since a *Book of Order* was first published in 1788.[3] This eighteenth-century phrase denotes what would today be called assumptions, or presuppositions, that undergird what follows. Chapter 1 is designed to be the "starting line" for reading the *Book of Order*. Attempting to understand the *Book of Order* without careful examination of this material is impracticable.

The Head of the Church (G-10100)

The *Book of Order* begins with G-1.0100, titled "The Head of the Church." Section G-1.0100a refers to Matt. 28:18 with one notable change. The word *authority*, which occurs in most translations, is rendered here as *power*. This uncommon presentation emphasizes the focus of this section, which is how Jesus Christ empowers the church. The first sentence of G-1.0100b begins, "Christ calls the Church into being, giving it all that is necessary for its mission to the world." This is a startling affirmation that may well spark discussion, yet it reminds us that this *Book of Order* is much more than a manual of operations for a human institution. An explanation of this assertion is found within the preamble to the "Rules of Discipline."

> The power that Jesus Christ has vested in his Church, a power manifested in the exercise of church discipline, is one for building up the body of Christ, not for destroying it, for redeeming, not for punishing. It should be exercised as a dispensation of mercy and not of wrath so that the great ends of the Church may be achieved, that all children of God may be presented faultless in the day of Christ. (D-1.0102)[4]

The section on "The Head of the Church" continues, giving added weight to the radical assertion that Christ is the head of the church.

Christ gives to his Church its faith and life, its unity and mission, its officers and ordinances. Insofar as Christ's will for the Church is set forth in Scripture, it is to be obeyed. In the worship and service of God and the government of the church, matters are to be ordered according to the Word by reason and sound judgment, under the guidance of the Holy Spirit. (G-1.0100c)

This introduces the scope of material in the *Book of Order*, which is nothing short of the human dimensions of church life. It also indicates that the basis for grasping Christ's intent for the church is Scripture. Beyond this, it is necessary that the church's life "be ordered according to the Word by reason and sound judgment, under the guidance of the Holy Spirit." Notice that sound judgment is not the same as independent, careful intellectual reflection on issues, but includes seeking the guidance of the Holy Spirit. This reminds us that polity as set forth in the *Book of Order* is understood as an essentially theological enterprise. It also underscores the importance of taking the *Book of Order* seriously.

The section on "The Head of the Church" ends with the affirmation that commitment to Jesus Christ as Lord includes confession of Christ as our hope and authority, which sets us free to glorify our Savior by living "in the lively, joyous reality of the grace of God." (G-1.0100d) So much for our *Book of Order* being dry and legal!

It is seldom noted that this theme of faith continues well beyond G-1.0000. Chapters 2 through 6 repeat the tone of chapter 1. The chapter on "Governing Bodies" (G-9.0103) begins its discussion of how the church is unified by restating G-1.0100c. One might be surprised that the *Book of Order* has so much theology in its pages. It is a historical reality that for Presbyterians, polity is the working out in practice of our understanding of discipleship to Christ.

The Great Ends of the Church (G-1.0200)

"Ends" as it appears in the section title, "The Great Ends of the Church," refers to the mission of the community called Christians. These six great ends or purposes provide a concise formulation of how we Presbyterians understand our mission as a church. This statement comes to us representing our heritage from the United Presbyterian Church of North America, which worked on it beginning in 1904 and finally adopted it in 1910.[5] The six "great ends" remind us that our mission as Presbyterians has always been multifaceted. They are delineated as:

1. the proclamation of the gospel for the salvation of humankind;

2. the shelter, nurture, and spiritual fellowship of the children of God;

3. the maintenance of divine worship;

4. the preservation of the truth;

5. the promotion of social righteousness; and

6. the exhibition of the kingdom of Heaven to the world.

The Report of the General Assembly Council to the 1997 General Assembly, in a paragraph that quotes the "great ends," offers the following exhortation.

> It sometimes seems that we get caught up in the details of our work, telling the story of how well we have carried out our responsibilities and lose sight of why we are doing what we do. These principles help us refocus on Jesus as the reason for mission as related in this report.[6]

This paragraph provides a concise answer for anyone who asks how Presbyterians understand their task as a church.[7] The "great ends" are also considered an important dimension of church discipline as outlined in the *Book of Order* (D-1.0101b), and have been used with communicants' classes, and in sessions' periodic review of how faithful local churches have been to their call.

The Historic Principles

In the next eight chapters, we will explore how the Historic Principles inform the *Book of Order*. There are some basic considerations to bear in mind as we proceed. Some may appear foolish or self-evident, but my experience suggests that they are worth noting.

Words in the *Book of Order* mean what they say. There are no hidden meanings. There are, however, complex relationships between provisions. It is sometimes difficult to grasp the basic meaning of the language since assumptions accumulated over the years tend to color understanding. To illustrate, the distinction between an elder and an elder in active service (currently serving on the session) is something to keep in mind when reading the first sentence of G-9.0203b.[8]

A Presbyterian vocabulary emerges in the *Book of Order*. There are words that have distinctive meanings, differing from common usage. There are terms that have dedicated meanings for specialized use. For example, a session meeting involves elders, but it is not a meeting of elders. The word *call*, which figures prominently in the *Book of Order*, is used in various ways depending on the context. This makes determining which sense is intended in a particular provision challenging, especially for those who are new to the book.

Words are understood in context. The *Book of Order* adds to this usual sense of context the assumption that what comes earlier in the text is more basic and more important than what comes later. Chapter 1 provides the framework for what follows. This means that there is a lot to be kept in mind when one works with the *Book of Order*, much as there is in the study of Scripture. It also means that to hunt for a specific sentence or provision to support what is already decided is to misuse the *Book of Order*. In this way, working with the *Book of Order* is similar to working with Scripture. To take specific provisions of a passage from the Bible without understanding where they fit in the overall picture may lead to distortion of what is being presented. If the *Book of Order* is taken as a law book, adherence to its provisions becomes onerous.

The approach being advocated in this study contends that the *Book of Order* is a theologically informed document representing the way a particular community of faith has worked out what it means to live together as a community of faith. As those who believe John 1:14 that "the Word became flesh and lived among us," we Presbyterians might expect that the text defining our polity would present tensions or polarities that are in and of themselves meaningful to people of faith. The logic of the *Book of Order* is the logic of faith, of the gospel, and of the incarnation. As these tensions are encountered, the need to bear in mind "the whole counsel of God," is highlighted.[9] To move from Scripture to *Confessions* to *Book of Order* is to change texts, but to remain in the same mode of interpretation.

The *Book of Order* is a theological document. The foundation of the *Book of Order* is Jesus Christ, who alone is the head of the church. That we have a Constitution that includes both a *Book of Confessions* and a *Book of Order* serves as an admonishment to Presbyterians to always remember that our life together in the church is based on the witness of Scripture, the *Book of Confessions,* and the *Book of Order*. We are called to be constitutional Presbyterians, and how we go about living our polity will demonstrate whether or not we are faithful to what we profess.

otes

1. The process for amending the *Book of Order* is set forth in G-18.0300.

2. 1. The Head of the Church (G-1.0100); 2. The Great Ends of the Church (G-1.0200); 3. The Historic Principles of Church Order (G-1.0300); 4. The Historic Principles of Church Government (G-1.0400); and 5. The Constitution Defined (G-1.0500).

3. The preface in the *Book of Church Order 1982–1983* of the Presbyterian Church (U.S.) is titled "Jesus Christ, the King and Head of the Church." In the *Book of Order 1982–1983* of the United Presbyterian Church in the United States of America, chapter 2 (after "Preliminary Principles") is titled "Of Jesus Christ, the Head of the Church."

4. This was added to the "Rules of Discipline" by both predecessor denominations in 1982. It was given its present numbering in the further modifications in 1995.

5. See footnote 2 of G-1.0200.

6. *Minutes of the 209th General Assembly* (1997), 30.0002, p. 205.

7. G-3.0000 provides further expansion of this theme.

8. The clerk of session must be an elder, but not necessarily an elder in active service. A clerk who is not a member of session would not have a vote in session meetings.

9. *Book of Confessions*, 6.006 (Westminster Confession 1:6).

2

Conscience and Community (G-1.0301)

Conscience is the guardian in the individual of the rules which the community has evolved for its own preservation.

—William Somerset Maugham, *The Moon and Sixpence*

Presbyterians talk a lot about conscience. Our commitment to the sanctity of conscience transcends lines that otherwise separate points of view. In this chapter we will consider where this conviction comes from, what are its roots, how conscience relates to the community of faith, and what the *Book of Order* says about conscience.

The first Historic Principle of Church Order (G-1.0301) raises the issue of conscience, indicating the importance of this topic. This first principle is the only one of the Historic Principles that has two parts. Part A quotes a sentence from the Westminster Confession, while part B interprets the quoted material.

The First Historic Principle (Part A)

God alone is Lord of the conscience, and hath left it free from the doctrines and commandments of men which are in anything contrary to his Word, or beside it, in matters of faith or worship.[1]

This is a theological affirmation that conscience, while deeply personal, is subject to the authority of God who is "Maker of all things, visible and invisible."[2] A theological affirmation such as this reminds us that we are dealing with something deeply personal, yet also subject to God as Lord. In this first phrase of the first Historic Principle, the relationship between God and God's creation is affirmed as fundamental. There is no hint here of an autonomous conscience that by itself can guide us through life's decisions. "Conscience" is understood by the writers to be the foundation for relating to God and to God's creation, including the rest of humankind. This statement warns that attempts to privatize conscience, as if it were the possession of an individual, are themselves denials of the basic affirmation that it is God who is Lord of the conscience, rather than the person in whom the conscience resides. God is the source of the sanctity of conscience, which, in turn, is to be upheld and defended against all attempts at coercion by the "powers of this world."

It is the relationship that is sacred, not conscience in and of itself. The Westminster Assembly and the church have subsequently understood conscience primarily as a theological, rather than psychological or sociological concept.

The Westminster Confession continues:

> So that to believe such doctrines, or to obey such commandments out of conscience, is to betray true liberty of conscience; and the requiring of an implicit faith, and an absolute and blind obedience, is to destroy liberty of conscience, and reason also.[3]

Typically, there are two aspects to a discussion of conscience. One is that to believe human doctrines and heed human commandments is to betray human freedom. The other is that it is inappropriate to require others to do so. Behind these convictions lies the English (and colonial American) history of those who dissented from the Anglican Church, being required to attend and support the official church, and being prohibited from preaching or worshiping where they wished.

This understanding of conscience has biblical roots, as well as historical salience. One root is the conviction arising from the first commandment (Ex. 20:3) that God is the Lord of all. The giving of the Ten Commandments formed God's covenant people out of what had, until then, been a disorganized and dispirited group of refugees. As a covenant people, they had a social boundary defined in various ways: initially by the Sinai code, then by allegiance to a king, and finally by parentage.

A second, New Testament root of the Presbyterian understanding of conscience relates to the controversy in the early church regarding membership in the "new" covenant community. The report of the council of Jerusalem in Acts 15 demonstrates the contentious nature of the issue of membership. Galatians 2:1–10 indicates that the Jerusalem solution recorded in Acts 15 did not end the dispute. Freedom, for the apostle Paul, is a major concern: "For freedom Christ has set us free!"[4] Paul, in his pastoral advice regarding whether it was permissible for a believer to eat meat that had been offered to idols, concludes that,

> "All things are lawful," but not all things are beneficial. "All things are lawful," but not all things build up. Do not seek your own advantage, but that of another. Eat whatever is sold in the meat market without raising any question on the ground of conscience. (1 Cor. 10:23–25)

He continues beyond this instruction, which initially seems so simple, to a more challenging point:

> But if someone says to you, "This has been offered in sacrifice," then do not eat it, out of consideration for the one who informed you, and for the sake of conscience—I mean the other's conscience, not our own. (1 Cor. 10:28–29)

Paul balances the importance of theological integrity with concern for others in the community who may hold different views. His counsel ends with an appeal to do everything out of joyous thankfulness to God.

Christian Maurer, discussing the Greek word συνοιδα (*synoida*), which is translated as "conscience" in the New Revised Standard Version, writes:

> Even though the verdict of conscience is positive, as Paul says in unparalleled fashion, it is not an autonomous verdict, but one based on God's Word.[5]

This sentence summarizes, in modern language, the quote from the Westminster Confession. While conscience is intensely personal, it is also one of our connections with the community in which we participate. Noted Presbyterian professor of religious education, C. Ellis Nelson, makes an important distinction between "negative conscience" (the internalization of regulatory authority that forms an unconscious code and precipitates guilt when violated), which is extremely moral and restrictive and of "positive conscience" (formed by the later internalization of principles by which parents live), which is more accessible, expansive, and open to education.[6] Nelson's contemporary social psychological understanding of conscience finds an interesting corollary in the Westminster Larger Catechism:

> **Q. 83.** What is the communion in glory with Christ, which the members of the invisible Church enjoy in this life?
> **A.** The members of the invisible Church have communicated to them, in this life, the first fruits of glory with Christ, as they are members of him their head, and so in him are interested in that glory which he is fully possessed of; and as an earnest thereof, enjoy the sense of God's love, peace of conscience, joy in the Holy Ghost, and hope of glory. As, on the contrary, the sense of God's revenging wrath, horror of conscience, and a fearful expectation of judgment, are to the wicked the beginning of the torment which they shall endure after death.[7]

The sharp distinction between a "peace of conscience" as a mark of blessedness on the one hand, and the "horror of conscience" for the "wicked" challenges a simple sociocultural understanding of conscience. Conscience is God's gift to humans to be used to God's glory. As with all gifts from God, we are stewards of the gift of conscience and, therefore, responsible for the use we make of it. The fellowship of faith nurtures this and God's other gifts in us. Together, we are better stewards than if we were left to our own individual understandings. Conscience belongs to us not as a sovereign possession, but as an internal reminder that we are integrally related to brothers and sisters, parents, and children in a web of mutual dependence. Conscience is the community internalized in each of us.[8]

In 1960, Rev. Maurice McCrackin was tried by the Permanent Judicial Commission of the General Assembly of the United Presbyterian Church in the United States of America regarding his position opposing the collection of taxes, which took the form of various actions of civil disobedience.[9] McCrackin appealed to freedom of conscience as his defense against the charges in the case. The opinion in the case cited the report of the Special Commission of 1925:

> If we can say on the one hand that conscience has its liberty, [we can also say] that liberty has its conscience. For Christ is lord of the man and the law as well as the lord of the man's conscience. We maintain that liberty of conscience and the law of the Church, in tension with each other under the authority of the Word of God, become the instrument of both the peace and the purity of the church.[10]

This ruling indicates that there is a tension between an individual's freedom of conscience and responsibility to civil law, which, in turn, generates important consequences for the life of the church.

A word search of the *Book of Order* locates fifteen references to the term *conscience*.[11] By looking at these references, we can see how the first Historic Principle informs the practices of Presbyterian church life.

The word *conscience* appears six times in chapter VI of the *Book of Order*, "The Church and Its Officers," in the discussion of "Offices of Ministry." Section G-6.0108 is made up of three paragraphs that deal with freedom of conscience. The section that provides what I consider the most important provision relating to a Presbyterian understanding of conscience is G-6.0108b, which reads:

> It is to be recognized, however, that in becoming a candidate or officer of the Presbyterian Church (U.S.A.) one chooses to *exercise freedom of conscience within certain bounds*. His or her conscience is captive to the Word of God as interpreted in the standards of the church so long as he or she continues to seek or hold office in that body. The decision as to whether a person has departed from essentials of Reformed faith and polity is made initially by the individual concerned but ultimately becomes the responsibility of the governing body in which he or she serves. (G-1.0301; G-1.0302; italics added)

The phrase "within certain bounds" makes the point that an individual's conscience is not sovereign for one who confesses that Jesus Christ is Lord. The next sentence provides a reminder that God's Word as interpreted in the *Book of Confessions* is the basis for the order Presbyterians have chosen for the church.[12] Officers are expected to adhere to this understanding of Christian faith.[13] While a person is responsible for compliance, the community of faith, through its governing bodies, is finally responsible for determining issues of conscience.[14] While this initially sounds intrusive, it also provides for the appropriate body to counsel an officer or candidate regarding whether the particular concern is truly at variance with Presbyterian convictions. An explicit reference to this role is found in G-9.0102b, where one of the powers given to all governing bodies is that they may "give counsel in matters of conscience."

The footnote to G-6.0108b elaborates on this last point. "Very early" in this footnote refers to a Plan of Union of 1758.[15] The three options outlined in that sentence, which is now 250 years old, have continued to define Presbyterian alternatives: "either actively concur with or passively submit. . . . or peaceably withdraw." This further underscores the tenet that conscience is not simply personal, but personal in the context of community. There is a significant sentence within the footnote that both limits and clarifies the situations in which these alternatives may come into play: "Provided always that this shall be understood to extend only to such determination as the body shall judge indispensable in doctrine or Presbyterian government." This provision provides protection against capricious application of these options, and should serve to limit rhetoric.

The *Book of Order* provides an avenue for protest by officers with troubled consciences.

> A protest is a written declaration, supported by reasons, expressing disagreement with what is believed by on or more members of a governing body to be an irregularity or a delinquency." (G-9.0304)

> If a protest is expressed in decorous and respectful language, the governing body shall enter it in its minutes in recognition of the person's right of conscience. That entry does not justify disobedience. (G-9.0304b)[16]

Section G-9.0305 carefully defines who may dissent or protest. On January 18, 1998, the attempt by the Presbytery of Milwaukee to "disobey" the amendment that added G-6.0106b to the *Book of Order* was ruled contrary to *Roberts' Rules of Order* and contrary to our Constitution, and hence was rendered ineffectual. This ruling was made by a Committee of Special Administrative Review of the Synod of Lakes and Prairies regarding the "Covenant of Dissent" of Milwaukee Presbytery.[17]

G-9.0304b highlights a distinction between the Presbyterian Church and our American legal system. That is that "Civil disobedience" as acts motivated by conscience are not appropriate in the Presbyterian Church. Advocacy in various forms short of acts contrary to the Constitution of the Presbyterian Church (U.S.A.) are expected.[18] Working for change may move some individuals to "ecclesiastical disobedience." When conscience moves one to intentional, extreme response, it should be done with an awareness that there may be short-term personal and possibly painful consequences. Here the *Book of Order* provides a reminder that the church is a voluntary organization that one may join and may also leave. There are provisions by which members and officers may peaceably withdraw from our fellowship. Conscience has a cost. For Presbyterians, conscience is neither a justification for defiance, nor an excuse for noncompliance. Presbyterians take conscience very seriously and respect those painful times when issues of conscience move some to seek other ways to fulfill their understanding of discipleship.

Two rulings by the Permanent Judicial Commission of the General Assembly (hereafter, GAPJC), provide glimpses into the important but delicate distinctions regarding matters of conscience. The first is the ruling on the case of *Buonaiuto vs. First Presbyterian Church*, Greenlawn, NY, in which the complainant-appellee had requested that the First Presbyterian Church, of which he was a member, not pay any per capita tax on his behalf to the Presbytery of Long Island.[19] After the case was considered at the presbytery and synod levels, appeal was made to the GAPJC. Their ruling is summarized as follows:

> Freedom of conscience and the right of protest do not give an individual church member the right to prevent a governing body from carrying out its responsibilities to another governing body.[20]

Another ruling had to do with the payment of per capita in the case of the *Session of Central Presbyterian Church vs. Presbytery of Long Island*.[21] In this case, the Session of Central Presbyterian Church of Huntington, New York, had voted to exercise their authority and refrain from participating in the per capita system because the General Assembly, the synod, and the presbytery had adopted policies and supported causes that they "no longer in good conscience" could "be a part of supporting." At a stated meeting, the presbytery responded by reaffirming its policy that any unpaid per capita be recorded as an outstanding obligation. The focus was thereby moved from the protest of the local congregation to the per capita system itself. Central Church responded by filing a formal complaint against the synod, charging that the presbytery had "encroached on the constitutional power of the session to 'determine the distribution of the church's benevolences' " (*Book of Order*, G-10.0102). The synod dismissed the complaint. The case was eventually appealed to the GAPJC, which issued a complex five-point ruling. The final two points can be summarized as follows:

4. Our system protects the rights of minority viewpoints, yet affirms the principle of majority rule. (G-1.0400)

5. While freedom of conscience is preserved, it is to be exercised within certain limits. There is a "duty of conscience" to support the ministry and mission of the church (G-6.0108b)[22]

The final reference to conscience in the *Book of Order* is found in the Directory of Worship in chapter III, section 4 , "The Sealing of the Word: Sacraments" in a section on administration of communion.

> The session is to determine what form of the fruit of the vine is to be used. In making this decision the session should be informed by the biblical precedent, the history of the church, ecumenical usage, local custom, and concerns for health and the conscience of members of the congregation. Whenever wine is used in the Lord's Supper, unfermented grape juice should always be clearly identified and served also as an alternative for those who prefer it. (W-3.3611)

Note that included among the six factors the session *should* consider is "concern for . . . the conscience of members of the congregation."[23] Here, conscience provides a potentially limiting factor to the decision of a session.

The First Historic Principle (Part B)

> Therefore we consider the rights of private judgment, in all matters that respect religion, as universal and unalienable: We do not even wish to see any religious constitution aided by the civil power, further than may be necessary for protection and security, and at the same time, be equal and common to all others. (G-1.0301b)

This second part of the first Historic Principle, which offers an interpretation of Part A, may seem to contradict aspects of the previous discussion. How can we affirm that the "rights of private judgment" are "universal and unalienable" and still hold that freedom of conscience is to be exercised "within certain bounds?"

The serious nature of the matter of the relief of conscience in Presbyterian Polity is evidenced in the *Book of Order* as it provides for a third form of relief, namely, renunciation of jurisdiction.

> When a church officer, whether a minister of the Word and Sacrament, elder, or deacon, renounces the jurisdiction of this church in writing to the clerk or stated clerk of the governing body of jurisdiction, the renunciation shall be effective upon receipt. Renunciation of jurisdiction shall remove the officer from membership and ordained office and shall terminate the exercise of office. (G-6.0500)

This two-sentence provision stands as the "conscience clause" in the *Book of Order*. The brevity of the paragraph understates the radical nature of this option. It is the one place where an officer is able, on one's own, to "leave the church." By writing a note, one may remove oneself from the Presbyterian Church (U.S.A.), no questions asked. This could be called the "Presbyterian ejection seat." Such is the allowance to the force of conscience, when one feels unable to continue as a Presbyterian officer.[24] The boundaries may be exceeded, but at considerable cost.

The final clause of the first Historic Principle, "We do not even wish to see any religious constitution aided by the civil power, further than may be necessary for protection and security, and at the same time, be equal and common to all others," represents an ecclesiastical endorsement of the First Amendment of the Constitution of the United States of America. This explicit endorsement of separation of church and state is reaffirmed in chapter IX of the *Book of Order*, "Governing Bodies."

> Governing bodies of the church are distinct from the government of the state and have no civil jurisdiction or power to impose civil penalties. They have only ecclesiastical jurisdiction for the purpose of serving Jesus Christ and declaring and obeying his will in relation to truth and service, order and discipline. (G-9.0102a)

It may seem odd that such a cherished principle of American government is restated at the point where governing bodies of the church are being defined. It apprises Presbyterians that the governing bodies of the Presbyterian Church (U.S.A.) are authoritative only in affairs of church life. Section G-9.0102a stands as a reminder of the limits of our decisions as we venture out in mission.

Such care regarding the relationship between church and state is also evident in chapters VII, "The Particular Church," and VIII, "The Church and Its Property." In chapter VII, phrases such as, "where civil law requires" (G-7.0403) and "unless the civil law provides otherwise" (G-7.0403b) serve to define how Presbyterians are to be faithful to the *Book of Order* and also to the laws of the various states that impact the governance of churches. In chapter VIII, the phrase "whenever permitted by civil law," modifies the call to incorporation (G-8.0202). Such provisions as these represent contemporary, practical applications of Jesus' teaching: "Give therefore to the emperor the things that are the emperor's and to God the things that are God's" (Matt. 22:21 and parallels). It is evident that care needs to be taken in regard to our understanding of the relationship between the church and civil government.

The *Book of Order* alerts us to the tension housed within the apparently simple concepts of "conscience" and "community." The tensions between these two concepts must be acknowledged if we are to live together productively as a church about our God's business. This tension must always be kept in what is a delicate balance. Attempts to destroy the tension by accentuating one aspect over the other will produce dislocation and distress. The quest for this balance has continued for over two centuries without a permanent resolution. In the midst of this tension lies the seeds of creativity for Presbyterians as we seek to be faithful to God in our own time.

It is also important to bear in mind that "community" for Presbyterians is a specific type of community. It is a *covenant* community. Presbyterians are part of a historic community that has its roots in the Mount Sinai community. This transhistorical community finds expression in a particular community meeting in a particular location at a particular point in history. The community itself is a sign that it is God who has called us into fellowship with one another. This is the community that forms our conscience, which reminds us who we are and whose we are. As Scripture puts it: "Once you were not a people, but now you are God's people" (1 Peter 2:10; see also Hos. 2:23).

Behind the conscience/community tension lies the question, "Why am I a Presbyterian?" The *Book of Order* reveals the assumption that the decision to join the Presbyterian Church (U.S.A.) is something that will be reviewed periodically. Changes in the *Book of Order* and the *Book of Confessions* may trigger questioning about continuing in the community of Presbyterians. Decisions in the session, presbytery, synod, or General Assembly may also stir up uncertainty. Each individual determines whether to accept changes as the will of a majority and continue in the community, or to follow his/her conscience in a quest for a more suitable community. These are not decisions that are appropriately made alone. By its nature, being Presbyterian involves a sense in which an individual's problem is better understood as a shared problem. Brother and sister Presbyterians are a spiritual resource for one another in the endeavor to grow as disciples of Jesus Christ. Being part of Presbyterian community means taking seriously the biblical admonition that "If one member suffers, all suffer together" (1 Cor. 12:26) as the essence of relationship within the community. Luther taught that we are, in fact, one another's priests. The attempt to solve one's problems of conscience in isolation is a denial of our being "members one of another" (Eph. 4:25).

The tension between conscience and community cautions us to be compassionate and caring when issues of conscience arise. Appeals to conscience are signals of deep pain within one of our sisters or brothers. Whether or not we are in agreement on issues of conscience, we have a duty to respond with consideration. Arguing matters of conscience is counter-productive, since pain and anger tend to short-circuit dialogue. The Constitution of the Presbyterian Church (U.S.A.) apprises us that as part of the community called by Christ, times of struggle over issues of conscience are times for caring and sensitivity.

Emerging from this study of the first Historic Principle is the suggestion that the transformed conscience is the engine of mission. "Positive conscience" is where God's Spirit enters into us in such a way that we *must* act on the basis of our conviction that Jesus Christ is Lord. Thus conscience is intimately related to living out our baptism. We will have opportunity to explore these mission implications in chapter 5 of this book.

otes

1. *Book of Confessions*, 6.109.

2. Ibid., 1.1.

3. Ibid., 6.109.

4. Gal. 5:1. Note that this comes in the middle of a paragraph.

5. Gerhard Friedrich, ed., *Theological Dictionary of the New Testament*, vol. VII (Grand Rapids, Michigan: Wm. B. Eerdmans Publishing Company, 1971), p. 916.

6. C. Ellis Nelson, *Don't Let Your Conscience Be Your Guide* (New York: Paulist Press, 1978), p. 28.

7. *Book of Confessions*, 7.193.

8. Of the twenty places where "conscience" occurs in the *Book of Confessions*, nine are in the Westminster Confession, and seven are in the Larger Catechism.

9. The decision against McCrackin was later reversed.

10. *The Presbyterian Constitution and Digest* (Louisville: Office of the General Assembly, 1963), p. A211b.

11. The references are as follows: G-1.0301, G-1.0307; G-6.0108 (a, b, and c, a total of six references); and W-3.3611. The other two instances are in footnotes in the Annotated Edition to G-5.0201 and G-10.0102, both are references to decisions of the Permanent Judicial Commission of the General Assembly. Note that the first reference is to another principle, dealing with attempts to "bind the conscience," which we will discuss in chapter 8.

12. See G-1.0100c; G-2.0200. See also *Book of Confessions*, 6.176.

13. See chapter 3.

14. This instruction is an implication of 1 Cor. 12:26: "If one member suffers, all suffer together with it." It also reflects serious and practical consideration of the Reformation principle of the priesthood of all believers.

15. For information regarding the context, see James H. Smylie, *A Brief History of the Presbyterians* (Louisville: Geneva Press, 1996), pp. 54–56.

16. Closely related to protest is *dissent*, which is a more modest response that expresses disagreement with an action or decision of a governing body (G-9.0303).

17. From www.lakesandprairies.org on January 26, 1998.

18. The church's Constitution builds on a decision of individuals, whereas the civil law is based on citizenship and residence.

19. *Buonaiuto vs. First Presbyterian Church*, Greenlawn, NY, in *Minutes of the 98th General Assembly* (1986), p. 158.

20. *Book of Order: Annotated Edition* (Louisville: Office of the General Assembly, 1997), G-5.202.

21. *Session of Central Presbyterian Church vs. Presbytery of Long Island*, in *Minutes of the 204th General Assembly (1992)*, p. 179.

22. It is important to note that while the decision is cited in G-10.0102 of the *Book of Order: Annotated Edition*, it underlines the significance and relevance of G-6.0108b.

23. The definition for the term *should* is provided in the preface to the *Book of Order* as "SHOULD signifies practice that is strongly recommended."

24. The distinction between members and officers will be covered in chapter 3.

3

$\mathscr{D}$efining the Boundaries (G-1.0302)

$\mathscr{T}$he second Historic Principle begins with an attention-getting phrase: "That, in perfect consistency with the above principle of common right. . . ." It is as if it were a directional sign leading the reader straight to a surprising and thought-worthy destination. The phrase reminds the reader that there is a careful connection between these first two principles. It also notifies the reader that he/she is about to see how the paradox of conscience and community are worked out in the social boundaries of community life.

The complex subject of G-1.0302 presents three levels of social institution: "every Christian Church, or union, or association of particular churches." This demonstrates an awareness of the diversity of polities in colonial America, as well as hinting at some of the complications that may arise from this situation. Such complexity introduces confusion regarding how to understand this principle. The key word here is the twice-used "or." "Every Christian Church" refers to those congregations who choose to be independent of other congregations.

"Association of particular churches" has to do with particular churches whose ties with other particular churches are loosely drawn, while a "union of particular churches" is a religious grouping where there are definite and lasting interconnections among the particular churches.

The historic development of Presbyterian churches moved from particular churches through the formation of presbyteries and synods, ending in 1789 with a General Assembly. It is axiomatic that to be Presbyterian is to be in a union of churches. This means that a particular Presbyterian church may not operate as an independent entity at variance with the provisions of the *Book of Order*.

Every religious community determines its own boundaries. Scope is the first matter a religious community needs to address. It requires setting both external and internal limits. It begins with a determination of what sort of relationship a given religious community will have with other religious communities.

The church where my wife and I worship (West Side Presbyterian Church, Ridgewood, New Jersey) has a dramatic stained-glass north window presenting Jesus as the Good Shepherd (a visual representation of

Matt. 18:10–11), who has just rescued a lost sheep and carries it in his arms. This scriptural image of Jesus as the Good Shepherd is balanced by John 10:1–18, where Jesus describes his role as shepherd to include gatekeeper as well as protector. The Council of Jerusalem (Acts 15) struggled with gate-keeping when it addressed whether Gentiles needed to be circumcised before they could become Christians. The gate-keeping function is the focus of the second Historic Principle.

Once the decision regarding external boundaries is made, according to the second Historic Principle, each cohesive community has to deal with three subordinate decisions.

> Every Christian Church . . . is entitled to declare the terms of admission into its communion and the qualifications of its ministers and members, as well as the whole system of its internal government which Christ hath appointed. (G-1.0302)

Each of these represents social boundaries that are important for any human social institution. Thus there is a "down-to-earth" realism in this principle that reminds us that "we have this treasure in clay jars" (2 Cor. 4:7). The Presbyterian Church (U.S.A.) is therefore defined as *part* (and only part) of the church of Jesus Christ.

Terms of Admission into Communion

"Terms of admission" is a phrase that arose during the Reformation within church bodies that were not state churches, where being a member was considered a part of living in a specific country or region. For most persons in Europe, admission into the church was through baptism in childhood. The free churches (those that were not supported by national taxes) had to determine the basis on which persons were admitted to their fellowships. Differences quickly emerged among free churches.

As early as 1561, it was necessary for the successor to Ulrich Zwingli, Heinrich Bullinger, to deal with the issue that, "Not all who are in the church are of the church."[1] He composed a document or personal confession that dealt with matters related to the Christian faith including the issue of membership, which he addressed, in part, through reference to Jesus' parables of the weeds in the field (Matt. 13:24–30) and of the net that catches all sorts of fish (Matt. 13:47–50). The document was accepted by the churches in Switzerland in 1566 as their new confession of faith and quickly found acceptance in European and non-European countries. It is now known as the Second Helvetic Confession and on the point of admission to fellowship it reads:

> We must not judge rashly or prematurely. Hence we must be very careful not to judge before the time, nor undertake to exclude, reject, or cut off those whom the Lord does not want to have excluded or rejected, and those whom we cannot eliminate without loss to the Church. On the other hand, we must be vigilant lest while the pious snore the wicked gain ground and do harm to the Church.[2]

The phenomenon of a "mixed" church was described in the Westminster Confession in 1646 using the terminology of a visible and invisible church.

1. The catholic or universal church, which is invisible, consists of the whole number of the elect, that have been, are, or shall be gathered into one, under Christ the head thereof; and is the spouse, the body, the fullness of Him that filleth all in all.[3]

2. The *visible* Church, which is also catholic or universal under the gospel (not confined to one nation as before under the law), consists of all those throughout the world that profess the true religion, together with their children; the house and family of God, through which men are ordinarily saved and union with which is essential to their best growth and service.[4]

After affirming that the visible church was given the "ministry, oracles, and ordinances of God,"[5] the Westminster Confession issues a sobering warning.

The purest churches under heaven are subject both to mixture and error: and some have so degenerated as to become apparently no churches of Christ. Nevertheless, there shall be always a Church on earth, to worship God according to his will.[6]

These quotes demonstrate how the necessity of determining who is admitted to fellowship in the church houses a paradox. No church is composed of purely "true" believers, yet there is "need for diligence" to protect the visible church from undue harm.

The *Book of Order* provisions on church membership build on these biblical and confessional foundations. Chapter V, "The Church and Its Members" opens as follows:

The incarnation of God in the life, death, and resurrection of Jesus Christ gives to the church not only its mission but also its understanding of membership. *One becomes an active member of the church* through faith in Jesus Christ as Savior and acceptance of his Lordship in all of life. Baptism and a public profession of faith in Jesus as Lord are the visible signs of entrance into the active membership of the church. (G-5.0101a; italics added)

Here is delineated the basis of membership: faith in Jesus Christ as Savior and acceptance of his Lordship in all of life. Two questions that are related to these conditions of membership are asked when a person desires to join a particular church.

The session has the responsibility of preparing persons who would become members of a given congregation (G-5.0401), for receiving members into a particular church (G-10.0102b), and for how the provisions of the *Book of Order* will be administered. At minimum, it is important for the session to provide new members with an understanding of how the church goes about its ministry.

Beyond such basic information, the *Book of Order* provides two possible foundations for organizing new member classes. The first possibility comes from the enumeration responsibilities of church membership that is found in (G-5.0102).

A faithful member accepts Christ's call to be involved responsibly in the ministry of his Church. Such involvement includes the following:

- proclaiming the good news;
- taking part in the common life and worship of a particular church;
- praying and studying Scripture and the faith of the Christian Church;
- supporting the work of the church through the giving of money, time, and talents;
- participating in the governing responsibilities of the church;
- demonstrating a new quality of life within and through the church;
- responding to God's activity in the world through service to others;
- living responsibly in the personal, family, vocational, political, cultural, and social relationships of life;
- working in the world for peace, justice, freedom, and human fulfillment (G-5.0102).

A session could use this list as a tool for evaluating what opportunities are provided for members to fulfill their responsibilities. In light of the importance of "informed consent," providing such a checklist to new members would concretize the responsibility that membership entails. Also, G-5.0500 calls for periodic review of membership.

Accepting the privilege and responsibility of membership in the church is a commitment to Jesus Christ that binds the individual to fulfillment of the obligations of membership. Members shall, when encouraged by the session, regularly review and evaluate the integrity with which they are involved in the ministry of the church and consider ways in which their participation in the worship and service of the church may be increased and made more meaningful. (G-5.0501)

Neglecting to mention the responsibilities of membership as new persons join the fellowship makes such evaluation virtually impossible.

As simple as this responsibility may seem to be, there are additional considerations. Within the description of an active member, there is the following clause:

Other conditions of active membership that meet the needs of the particular church and are consistent with the order and confessions of the Presbyterian Church (U.S.A.) may be adopted by the session after careful study and discussion with the congregation. (G-5.0202)

Note how carefully the process of implementing other conditions is designed in order to provide opportunity for careful reflection and inclusion of the whole community.

Another possibility for a full disclosure orientation might be drawn from the covenant for organizing a particular church given in chapter VII, "The Particular Church." The second sentence of the covenant might serve well as part of the public reception of new members.

> We promise and covenant to live together in unity and to work together in ministry as disciples of Jesus Christ, bound to him and to one another as a part of the body of Christ in this place according to the principles of faith, mission, and order of the Presbyterian Church (U.S.A.). (G-7.0201)

In the contemporary context of persons moving from place to place and of a diversity of persons joining Presbyterian Churches, such a declaration provides the opportunity to ensure that new members understand that:

> The law and government of the Presbyterian Church (U.S.A.) presuppose the fellowship of women and men with their children in voluntary covenanted relationship with one another and with God through Jesus Christ. The organization rests upon the fellowship and is not designed to work without trust and love. (G-7.0103)

This covenant underscores the importance of how a denomination chooses to govern itself.

Qualifications of Ministers

Qualifications for ministers is an important social boundary to which chapters VI, "The Church and Its Officers," and XIV, "Ordination, Certification and Commissioning," of the *Book of Order* are dedicated. Ordination is the term Presbyterians use regarding offices of ministry. The Presbyterian understanding of ordination is set forth in "Ordination for Church Office."

> The persons elected by the church to service in the offices of the church [G-6.0000] shall be ordained to these offices by the church. Ordination is the act by which the church sets apart persons to be presbyters (ministers of the Word and Sacrament or elders) or deacons, and is accompanied with prayer and the laying on of hands. Ordination to the office of minister of the Word and Sacrament is an act of the presbytery. Ordination to the offices of elder and deacon is an act of the session, except in the case of the organization of a new church. (G-7.0202; G-14.0101)

Ordination is by the "church to service in the offices of the church." The key word for understanding ordination is "service."

> The purpose and pattern of leadership in the church in all its forms of ministry shall be understood not in terms of power but of service, after the manner of the servant ministry of Jesus Christ. (G-14.0103)

The biblical warrant for this is extensive. It includes the Servant Songs of Isaiah (42:1–4; 49:1–6; 50:4–9; and 52:13—53:12) and is pointedly evident in John 13:1–15 where Jesus washes the disciples' feet. Further clarification of this servant metaphor is found in the description of offices of ministry in chapter VI.

> One responsibility of membership in the church is the election of officers who are ordained to fulfill particular functions. The existence of these offices in no way diminishes the importance of the commitment of all members to the total ministry of the church. These ordained officers differ from other members in function only. (G-6.0102)

All members are expected to engage in some sort of ministry. The stress is on the *function* of ministry, which is a hallmark of Reformed polity. John Calvin drew on the imperatives of Matt. 28:19 ("Go," "baptize") as basis for a functional understanding of church office.

Another characteristic of Presbyterian officers is that there is equality among *presbyters*. As presbyters, Ministers of Word and Sacrament and elders have equal votes in governing bodies above the session. *Presbyter* is a transliteration of a Greek word meaning "elder," which refers to an ancient office.[7] There is a delineation of the qualifications of an elder in 1 Tim. 3:1–7 as well as Titus 1:5–9. These references have been used historically in support of the role of the elder. The Reformed stream noted that the other major official term for a church leader is επισκοπος (*episcopos*) or bishop that appears in Acts 20:28 as an address to the elders from Ephesus (compare v. 18).[8]

A final attribute of Presbyterian understanding of officers is a three-part *call* to office. The three parts can be identified as inner or extraordinary call, external or ordinary call, and call of God's people.[9]

> To those called to exercise special functions in the church—deacons, elders, and ministers of the Word and Sacrament—God gives suitable gifts for their various duties. In addition to possessing the necessary gifts and abilities, natural and acquired, those who undertake particular ministries should be persons of strong faith, dedicated discipleship, and love of Jesus Christ as Savior and Lord. Their manner of life should be a demonstration of the Christian gospel in the church and in the world. They must have the approval of God's people and the concurring judgment of a governing body of the church. (G-6.0106a)[10]

The process for approving elders and ministers of Word and Sacrament will be discussed more fully in the next chapter.

The Whole System of Internal Government

The phrase "whole system of its internal government" suggests all the contents of the *Book of Order*, which is the subject of this study. However, there is a summary dating from 1797 that came to be called the "radical" principles of Presbyterian church government that appear in G-1.0400.[11] A detailed treatment of these principles appears in chapter 10.

The Consequences of Decisions

The second Historic Principle celebrates the self-determination that led to the writing of the Declaration of Independence and the Constitution of the U.S.A. The drafters of the Historic Principles were extending the concept of self-governance from the formation of a republic to the emergence of church bodies. The issue of consequences of erroneous decisions was debated strenuously. Such is the context of the second Historic Principle, which places in perspective its final phrase.

> That in the exercise of this right they may, notwithstanding, err, in making the terms of communion either too lax or too narrow; yet, even in this case, they do not infringe upon the liberty or the rights of others, but only make an improper use of their own.

An inherent risk in self-determination is that of making unwise decisions. Acknowledgement of this danger is included within the second Historic Principle, and two centuries of Presbyterian self-governance in this country testify to the continuing wisdom of its inclusion. Many decisions in the life of the church involve the dilemma of being "too lax or too narrow." Church officers quickly learn that what seems right at one time may later seem wrong. What is often troublesome is how unfortunate consequences of decisions may arise at a later time. The well-known saying "to err is human" applies directly to life in the church.

The final phrase of the second Historic Principle draws the amazing conclusion that when a body makes a bad decision, "they do not infringe upon the liberty or the rights of others, but only make an improper use of their own." This is a sobering reminder that responsibility for the consequences of a decision rest on the ones who make the choice.

What is the background for this assertion? One possible foundation is the drafters' understanding of Jesus' warning in Matt. 18:6: "If any of you put a stumbling block before one of these little ones who believe in me, it would be better for you if a great millstone were fastened around your neck and you were drowned in the depth of the sea." The warning follows Jesus' teaching about the importance of being childlike and in so doing highlights the consequences of rejecting the sort of acceptance Jesus practiced.[12]

A dilemma arises when it is noted that there are instances in the New Testament where a more careful approach to the boundaries of fellowship is indicated. In 1 Cor. 6:9, Paul asks the fellowship, "Do you not know that wrongdoers will not inherit the kingdom of God?" He then goes on to list some examples of the sort of people he considers unsuitable for Christian fellowship. Although this dilemma is not new, it is not any easier in the contemporary church. The second Historic Principle makes the setting of social boundaries a matter of stewardship. We are responsible for the decisions we make and for how we make them. Rather than being a sober task, however, we might recall that stewardship is an expression of Christian freedom through which we seek to honor our Lord with our faithfulness. This characterization is reflected in chapter IV of the *Book of Order*, "The Church and Its Unity," under the heading of "Principles of Presbyterian Government."

> Presbyters are not simply to reflect the will of the people, but rather to seek together to find and represent the will of Christ. (G-4.0301d)

We are called to do the best we can, using our abilities to God's glory, as we seek to express our thanksgiving to God for the blessings of life and faith. On this note, then, we turn to the third Historic Principle and the matter of officers for the church.

otes

1. *Book of Confessions*, 5.139.

2. Ibid., 5.140.

3. Ibid., 6.140.

4. Ibid., 6.141.

5. Ibid., 6.143.

6. Ibid., 6.144. Note in the footnotes to this section how the wording has been softened since 1647.

7. The article on πρεσβυτερος (*presbuteros*) by Gunter Bornkamm in *Theological Dictionary of the New Testament*, edited by Gerhard Friedrich, vol. VI (Grand Rapids: Wm. B. Eerdmans Publishing Co., 1968), pp. 651–680, gives the history of the role of elders in the Old Testament, as well as the usage of the term in the New Testament, and by the early church fathers. The account in Num. 11:16 and following suggests how Moses modified the traditional role of the elders.

8. This point is made by Hermann Beyer in *Theological Dictionary of the New Testament*, vol. II, p. 616. Beyer notes the word is Greek in origin, which may account for the different usage in the early church.

9. This distinction can be traced to John Calvin, *Institutes of the Christian Religion*, edited by John T. McNeill and translated by Ford Lewis Battles (Philadelphia: The Westminster Press, 1960), IV.III., pp. 1062 and 1066. The same scheme is found in Andrew Melville, *The Second Book of Discipline* (1578), and is found in David W. Hall and Joseph H. Hall, ed., *Paradigms in Polity* (Grand Rapids: Wm. B. Eerdmans Publishing Company, 1994), p. 237.

10. The phrase "manner of life" will be discussed in chapter 4.

11. The footnote to G-1.0400 defines *radical* as "fundamental and basic."

12. The saying appears also in Luke 17:2 in the same context, while in Mark 9:38–42 the saying follows the disciples' report of someone casting out demons in Jesus' name.

4

Church Officers (G-1.0303)

Why Church Officers?

The first annual meeting I attended as a church member taught me about officers. We met in the basement of the North Presbyterian Church of Lansing, Michigan. The new pastor, who displayed strong leadership tendencies, made a ruling in the middle of the meeting to which a distinguished elder objected, correcting the pastor by quoting a provision of the *Book of Order*. The pastor accepted the correction, and the meeting continued. I remember thinking that a church where an elder would correct the pastor with a *Book of Order* was my sort of church.

It can properly be said that Martin Luther began the Protestant Reformation when he began to teach the doctrine of the priesthood of all believers. This hallmark of the Reformation soon came to be misunderstood as "everyone their own priest," while Luther's position was "everyone a priest for their brother and sister."[1] What Luther intended was that each person would be a "priest" for his/her neighbor, assuming responsibility for the vitality of faith beyond one's own. From this early misunderstanding of theological equality as the basis for individualism arose the position that there was no need for officers in the church.[2] This position is widely held among church people today.

Heinrich Bullinger made an important distinction when he presented the following interpretation of "the priesthood of all believers," in what became the Second Helvetic Confession.

> *Priesthood of All Believers.* To be sure, Christ's apostles call all who believe in Christ "priests," but not on account of an office, but because, all the faithful having been made kings and priests, we are able to offer up spiritual sacrifices to God through Christ (Ex. 19:6; 1 Pet. 2:9; Rev. 1:6). Therefore, the priesthood and the ministry are very different from one another. For the priesthood, as we have just said, is common to all Christians; not so is the ministry. Nor have we abolished the ministry of the Church because we have repudiated the papal priesthood from the Church of Christ.[3]

This surprising move, which is consistent with Luther's position, makes priesthood a ministry for all believers. This passage shows a reversal of contemporary use of "priest" and "ministry." The emphasis is on our priestly responsibility to one another to a sobering, almost breathtaking degree.

When considered in the context of controversy over whether or not there should be officers, and how, if they exist, they should be designated, the force of the third Historic Principle becomes striking.

> That our blessed Savior, for the edification of the visible Church, which is his body, hath appointed officers, not only to preach the gospel and administer the Sacraments, but also to exercise discipline, for the preservation of both truth and duty; and that it is incumbent upon these officers, and upon the whole Church, in whose name they act, to censure or cast out the erroneous and scandalous, observing, in all cases, the rules contained in the Word of God. (G-1.0303)

This principle expands on the expression in G-1.0100c that "Christ gives to his Church . . . its officers . . ." It may be surprising to think of officers as Christ's gift to the church. The three functions mentioned—preach the gospel, administer the sacraments, administer discipline—echo the "marks of the church" as identified in the Scots Confession.

> The notes of the true Kirk, therefore, we believe, confess, and avow to be: first, the true preaching of the Word of God, in which God has revealed himself to us, as the writings of the prophets and apostles declare; secondly, the right administration of the sacraments of Christ Jesus, with which must be associated the Word and promise of God to seal and confirm them in our hearts; and lastly, ecclesiastical discipline uprightly ministered, as God's Word prescribes, whereby vice is repressed and virtue nourished.[4]

It is thus evident that Christ's purpose in giving the gift of officers is, as the third Historic Principle states, "for the edification of the visible Church, which is [our blessed savior's] body." This is a reminder of the New Testament image of the church as the body of Christ (Rom. 12:3–8; 1 Cor. 12:12–30; and Eph. 4:4–16), which emphasizes diverse functions within oneness in Christ.

This principle alerts us to the importance of mission, as it is discussed in chapter III of the *Book of Order*, "The Church and Its Mission." Here are found expressions worthy of wider use than they usually enjoy. Some of the brief sentences could, in fact, be used as foundational texts for sermons or educational endeavors. These statements are exciting and challenging, traits perhaps not anticipated in the *Book of Order*. Some examples are the following:

- The mission of the Church is given form by God's activity in the world as told in the Bible and understood by faith. (G-3.0100)

- The Church of Jesus Christ is the provisional demonstration of what God intends for all of humanity. (G-3.0200)

- The Church is called to be Christ's faithful evangelist . . . (G-3.0300c)

- The Church is called to undertake this mission even at the risk of losing its life, trusting in God alone . . . (G-3.0400)

• The Church is called to a new openness . . . (G-3.0401a–d)

These five statements provide a picture of the mission Jesus Christ has given the church. Study of chapter III could serve as a way to evaluate how faithful a given congregation is to its mission, and to identify areas for improvement. Such consideration also challenges officers in a governing body to review where they have not yet fulfilled Christ's call to mission, and to determine how they can bring themselves and the congregation into compliance with our corporate call.

The centrality of mission in the Presbyterian understanding of faith is further indicated by 121 instances of the word *mission* in the *Book of Order*.[5] Curiously, there are only fourteen instances of the word *mission* in the *Book of Confessions*. All appear in the Confession of 1969 and most are found as part of the phrase, "mission of reconciliation."[6] This paucity of instances in our confessional literature reflects the emergence of mission as a key word for Reformed churches in the late nineteenth century.[7]

The introduction of mission prior to a discussion of church offices places mission in its proper position as an essential aspect of church life. Mission frequently gets lost in the details of church life, or suffers from being only partially understood. G-3.0000 makes the point that officers are responsible to see that the church in their care gets on with mission. This is the Presbyterian version of the "prime directive." It is also a reminder that the church necessarily differs from the society in which it finds itself.

Which Church Officers?

The third Historic Principle catalogs the functions of officers but does not specify which officers should be appointed. Which officers the congregations within Presbyterian Church (U.S.A.) will have is spelled out in chapter VI, "The Church and Its Officers."

> The Church offices mentioned in the New Testament which this church has maintained include those of presbyters (ministers of the Word and Sacrament and elders) and deacons. (G-6.0103)

The answer to the question, "What officers does the Presbyterian Church (U.S.A.) have?" is simply presbyters and deacons.

The parentheses in G-6.0103 indicate that the office of presbyter has two components: Ministers of the Word and Sacrament, and elders, highlighting the equality between ministers of the Word and Sacrament and elders. As presbyters, each has an equal vote in governing bodies of the Presbyterian church. This distinctive parity also indicates that Presbyterians do not have clergy or laity. Rather the distinction is between officers and members. It is the responsibility of the membership to elect officers who are ordained to fulfill particular functions. The distinction between officers and members is clarified as follows:

> The existence of these offices in no way diminishes the importance of the
> commitment of all members to the total ministry of the church. These ordained
> officers differ from other members in function only. (G-6.0102)

Herein lies another Presbyterian concept. Ordination is to function, that is to
build up and extend the body of Christ, rather than to status. This
understanding of ordination accentuates the belief that mission is more
important than status.

The Confession of 1967 provides a pointed statement about how the
church goes about ordering its life.

> The church thus orders its life as an institution with a constitution, government,
> officers, finances, and administrative rules. These are instruments of mission, not
> ends in themselves. Different orders have served the gospel, and none can claim
> exclusive validity. A presbyterian polity recognizes the responsibility of all
> members for ministry and maintains the organic relation of all congregations in the
> church. It seeks to protect the church from exploitation by ecclesiastical or secular
> power and ambition. Every church order must be open to such reformation as may
> be required to make it a more effective instrument of the mission of reconciliation.[8]

This section of the confession stands as a witness to the need for the
organization of a church, while recognizing the potential for exploitation
within the fellowship.

Thus mutuality of officers serving Christ and the church is a hallmark of
Presbyterian polity.[9] The most succinct statement of this collegiality is found in
chapter X, "The Session."

> The session of a particular church consists of the pastor or co-pastors, the associate
> pastors, and the elders in active service. All members of the session, including the
> pastor, co-pastors, and associate pastors, are entitled to vote. (G-10.0101)

In 1993, the Report of a Special Committee on the Nature of the Church and
the Practice of Governance put forth, and the General Assembly approved,
among other recommendations, a restatement of G-10.0101.

> Pastors and elders together as the session are to govern with an emphasis on the
> shared responsibility of ministers of the Word and Sacrament and elders.[10]

The complexity of living out this shared responsibility is demonstrated in
the discussion of "Responsibility and Accountability for Worship," found
within "The Directory for Worship." There is a paragraph on session
responsibility (W-1.4004), responsibility of the minister as pastor (W-1.4005),
and then session and pastor (W-1.4006). The words in these paragraphs have
been chosen with great care and require careful reading and thoughtful
discussion to avoid misunderstandings of the roles and responsibilities of the
session and pastor in providing for the worship of a particular church.

Who Should Be a Church Officer?

When discussing who should be a church officer, it is important to distinguish between eligibility and call. G-6.0105 begins, "Both men and women shall be eligible to hold church offices," making it clear that gender is no bar to service as an officer in the Presbyterian Church (U.S.A.).[11] This distinction between eligibility and call is indicated in the Confession of 1967.

> In recognition of special gifts of the Spirit and for the ordering of its life as a community, the church calls, trains, and authorizes certain members for leadership and oversight. The persons qualified for these duties in accordance with the polity of the church are set apart by ordination or other appropriate act and thus made responsible for their special ministries. (C-9.39)

The phrase, "calls, trains, and authorizes" provides an explanation of how the process works, bringing us once again to the Reformed understanding of the three-part call. Table 1 identifies the components of call and where they are discussed in the *Book of Order*. It also points out the parallel structure that exists for Ministers of Word and Sacrament and elders.

TABLE 1. OVERVIEW OF PRESBYTERIAN ORDINATION

Aspect	Minister of Word & Sacrament	Elder
Inner call	Personal sense, appropriate gifts (G-6.0105–0106; 14.0300)	Personal sense, appropriate gifts (G-6.0105–0106)
Call of God's people	Call to service (G-14.0401)	G-14.0204
Governing body Confirmation	Examination by presbytery (G-14.0400)	G-14.0205

This parallel structure is also evident in the questions asked of those to be ordained as Ministers of Word and Sacrament (G-14.0405b) and as elders or deacons (G-14.0207). The only difference is the final question, which reflects specific functions related to each office.

Admittedly, there is a lot more material regarding Ministers of Word and Sacrament than elders and deacons in G-14.0000. This may seem to run counter to the concept of parity. One reason for this disparity may be that elders and deacons work mostly in groups, whereas Ministers of Word and Sacrament function largely alone, in the sense that they are responsible for regular worship and preaching, as well as seeing that the polity of the church is upheld.

The third aspect of call—that of confirmation by a governing body— highlights the paradox inherent in the Presbyterian theology of call. The word *call* appears within the *Book of Order*, forty-three times in "Form of Government" and twenty-one times in the "Directory for Worship," in reference to a variety of actions including God's call in Christ to individuals and the process by which churches and pastors find one another. This richness of meaning is also reflected in the concept of call as it appears in Scripture and the Confessions.[12] The tension lies in the fact that not everyone who feels called to ministry as an officer of the church will be validated for service by the church. Personal experience of calling is not, by itself, accepted as a validation within the Presbyterian Church (U.S.A.).

As noted in chapter 3 of this book, of discussing the requirements for church officers, G-6.0106 uses the curious phrase, "manner of life." The phrase alludes to what is expressed in the Second Helvetic Confession as:

> Not any one may be elected, but capable men distinguished by sufficient consecrated learning, pious eloquence, simple wisdom, lastly, by moderation and an honorable reputation, according to that apostolic rule which is compiled by the apostle in 1 Tim., ch. 3, and Titus, ch. 1.[13]

"Manner of life" has generated much discussion and debate since 1978, when the General Assembly responded to a 1976 overture from the presbyteries of New York City and Palisades requesting "definitive guidance" regarding ordination of candidates for the ministry otherwise qualified, "but who affirm their own homosexual identity and practice." The response of the 190th General Assembly of the United Presbyterian Church in the United States of America was,

> That unrepentant homosexual practice does not accord with the requirements of ordination set forth in Form of Government VII, Section 3 (37.03): . . . It is indispensable that, besides possessing the necessary gifts and abilities, natural and acquired, everyone undertaking a particular ministry should have a sense of inner persuasion, be sound in faith, life according to godliness, have the approval of God's people and the concurring judgment of a lawful judiciary of the Church.[14]

Recommendations 6 and 8 (there were 14 recommendations) of the response sought to provide the definitive guidance that the two presbyteries had requested.

> 6. Urges candidates committees, personnel committees, nominating committees, and judicatories to conduct their examination of candidates for ordained office with discretion and sensitivity, recognizing that it would be a hindrance to God's grace to make specific inquiry into the sexual orientation or practice of candidates for ordained office or ordained officers where the person involved has not taken the initiative in declaring his or her sexual orientation.

8. Calls on United Presbyterians to reject in their own lives, and challenge in others, the sin of homophobia, which drives homosexual persons away from Christ and his church.[15]

That the "definitive guidance" and recommendations did not settle the issue is shown by the fact that there have been sixteen actions since then. Between 1978 and 1998, there has been one approved amendment[16] and four rejected amendments to the *Book of Order*; two requests rejected; three subsequent interpretations; and three cases decided by the Permanent Judicial Commission of the General Assembly regarding issues of sexual orientation related to ordination.[17] Similar "definitive guidance" has been offered throughout our history regarding various practices, deemed sins, such as drinking "ardent spirit" and the use of tobacco.[18] In these earlier cases, the consequence was the denial of scholarship money from the denomination's agencies to recalcitrant persons. It is also the case that in such instances, later actions removed the restrictions. It is too early to determine what effect G-6.0106b will have on the church.

The third Historic Principle closes with a condition fundamental to Presbyterian polity that must not be overlooked because it is at the end.

. . . observing, in all cases, the rules contained in the Word of God. (G-1.0303)

A paradox arises when we seek together to interpret "the rules contained in the Word of God." How do Presbyterians simultaneously remain faithful to Scripture while also affirming that

the church, in obedience to Jesus Christ, is open to the reform of its standards of doctrine as well as of governance. The church affirms *Ecclesia reformata, semper reformanda*, that is, "The church reformed, always reforming," according to the Word of God and the call of the Spirit. (G-2.0200)

In an increasingly diverse denomination, doing so requires ongoing discussion and care. This issue will be treated more thoroughly in chapter 6 of this book.

otes

1. Andreas Carlstadt in 1521 was the first to implement a thorough-going social egalitarianism as an extension of Luther's "priesthood of all believers." Luther subsequently repudiated this view. Roland H. Bainton, *The Reformation of the Sixteenth Century* (Boston: Beacon Press, 1952,) pp. 65–66.

2. The "leveling" ended hierarchical distinctions between clergy and laity, which surprisingly persists in the language of many church folk. For the importance of the ending of hierarchy by Luther, and for an insight that continues to challenge prevalent understandings, see Paul Tillich, *Systematic Theology*, vol. III (Chicago: The University of Chicago Press, 1963), p. 13.

3. *Book of Confessions*, 5.153.

4. Ibid., 3.18.

5. There are a hundred occurrences of the word *mission* in the "Form of Government," and twenty-one in the "Directory for Worship."

6. One instance appears in the preliminary material of the Barmen Declaration.

7. An indication of this is the addition of a chapter to the Westminster Confession of Faith "Of the Gospel of the Love of God and Missions" in 1903. This chapter appears both as 6.055–058 and 6.187–190 in the *Book of Confessions.*

8. *Book of Confessions*, 9.40.

9. Further discussion of this issue is found in chapter 8.

10. *Minutes of the 205th General Assembly, 1993*, p. 381. The full report is on pp. 355–398.

11. See A Brief Statement of Faith, *Book of Confessions*, 10.4, line 64. This is a step beyond the Confession of 1967 (9.38–39), which uses a masculine pronoun, reflecting the language of the time. Still, this is a small indicator of the slowness of progress in the area of gender equality.

12. There are twenty-six instances of the word *call* in the *Book of Confessions.*

13. *Book of Confessions*, 5.150. The context of this paragraph in the Second Helvetic Confession includes the two preceding paragraphs: 5.148, "Papal Orders;" and 5.149, "Concerning Monks." Reformers were particularly aware of what they were responding to in the life of the Church. See also John Calvin, *Institutes of the Christian Religion*, edited by John T. McNeill and translated by Ford Lewis Battles (Philadelphia: The Westminster Press, 1960), Book IV.XIII, paragraphs 11, 13. The reference to 1 Timothy 3 and Titus 1 reminds us that this has been a long-standing concern for the church.

14. *Minutes of the 198th General Assembly* (1986), pp. 1023–1024. This is a reprinting of the original response given in 1978.

15. *Recommendations* 6 and 8, Ibid., p. 1024.

16. G-6.0106b in 1997.

17. Notes to G-6.0106 in the *Book of Order: Annotated Edition* (Louisville: Office of the General Assembly, 1997).

18. *The Presbyterian Constitution and Digest* (Louisville: Office of the General Assembly, 1968), pp. A979–A984. "Ardent spirit" actions were from 1811 to 1880. Tobacco action was in 1916.

5

*F*aith, Truth, and Mission (G-1.0304)

*A*fter reading its first two chapters, a seminary student exclaimed, "I never expected to find theology in the *Book of Order*." I was delighted to hear that a first class in Presbyterian polity had stimulated this discovery. It might be disturbing that a second-year seminary student would just be finding this out, but even more sobering is the reality that many who use the *Book of Order* in the life of the church forget what the seminarian discovered—that there is indeed theology in the *Book of Order*.

The paradox that the fourth Historic Principle presents is as old as the question, "How can we recognize a word that the LORD has not spoken?" (Deut. 18:17–22), and as recent as current newspaper accounts of someone claiming to be a prophet. Jesus warns the disciples about false prophets: "Not everyone who says to me, 'Lord, Lord,' will enter the kingdom of heaven" (Matt. 7:15–20). How can faithful disciples evaluate the truthfulness of church teachings?

The fourth Historic Principle provides, with carefully chosen language and delicately crafted logic, a way of approaching the dilemma of determining religious validity.

> That truth is in order to goodness; and the great touchstone of truth, its tendency to promote holiness, according to our Savior's rule, "By their fruits ye shall know them." And that no opinion can be either more pernicious or more absurd than that which brings truth and falsehood upon a level, and represents it as of no consequence what a man's opinions are. On the contrary, we are persuaded that there is an inseparable connection between faith and practice, truth and duty. Otherwise, it would be of no consequence either to discover truth or to embrace it. (G-1.0304)

At the outset, one might be surprised, if not bewildered, by the eighteenth-century English phrase, "in order to." In contemporary usage, "in order to" is a way of introducing purpose or sequence. It makes better sense for the modern reader to say, "That truth is on the same order as goodness." But the heart of the fourth Historic Principle lies not in these opening words but in its brilliant braiding of belief and action. This principle is about truth, faith, and mission. In our examination of it, we will begin by exploring the concepts of truth, goodness, faith, and holiness. We will then ponder how this principle affects the way mission is understood for the church and for individual Christians.

The word *truth* appears several times in the *Book of Confessions*. The Scots Confession reads:

> Our faith and its assurance do not proceed from flesh and blood, that is to say, from the natural powers within us, but are the inspiration of the Holy Ghost; whom we confess to be God, equal with the Father and with his Son, who sanctifies us into all the truth by his own working, without whom we should remain forever enemies to God and ignorant of his Son, Christ Jesus.[1]

There is an allusion here to Jesus' promise in John 15 that the Advocate or Helper will come—"the Spirit of truth [who] will guide you into all truth" (v. 13).

The word *truth* appears four times in the Second Helvetic Confession. First, there is a citation of John 14:26.

> When the Counselor comes, whom I shall send to you from the Father, even the Spirit of truth, who proceeds from the Father, he will bear witness to me.[2]

Next there is reference to John 4:2ff.

> We teach that God is to be adored and worshiped as he himself has taught us to worship, namely, "in spirit and in truth," not with any superstition, but with sincerity, according to His Word.[3]

Third, there is reference to John 1:17.

> The Gospel is, indeed, opposed to the law. For the law works wrath and announces a curse, whereas the Gospel preaches grace and blessing. John says: "For the law was given through Moses; grace and truth came through Jesus Christ" (John 1:17).[4]

Finally, there is reference to 1 Tim. 2:4.

> But because God from the beginning would have men to be saved, and to come to a knowledge of the truth (1 Tim. 2:4), it is altogether necessary that there always should have been, and should be now, and to the end of the world, a Church.[5]

These citations from the Gospel of John and 1 Timothy define *truth* in reference to the truth of Jesus Christ, who is the way, the truth, and the life (John 14:6). In addition, the last instance hints at the mission implications within the concept of truth. Evangelical truth, the truth of Jesus Christ, the Word made flesh, is truth with a built-in dynamic.

The theological connection between truth and mission is reinforced in the Shorter Catechism in its treatment of "justifying faith," and "assurance of salvation."

Justifying faith is a saving grace, wrought in the heart of a sinner, by the Spirit and the Word of God; whereby he, being convinced of his sin and misery, and of the disability in himself and all other creatures to recover him out of his lost condition, not only assenteth to the truth of the promise of the gospel, but receiveth and resteth upon Christ and his righteousness therein held forth, for pardon of sin, and for the accepting and accounting of his person righteous in the sight of God for salvation.

Such as truly believe in Christ, and endeavor to walk in all good conscience before him, may, without extraordinary revelation, by faith grounded upon the truth of God's promises, and by the Spirit enabling them to discern in themselves those graces to which the promises of life are made, and bearing witness with their spirits that they are the children of God, be infallibly assured that they are in the estate of grace, and shall persevere therein unto salvation.[6]

The concept of truth, as defined in the confessions, indicates that the fourth Historic Principle is concerned with living as faithful disciples. The confessions link growth as disciples to the capacity do good things, as the Second Helvetic Confession instructs:

In regard to goodness and virtue, man's reason does not judge rightly of itself concerning divine things. For the evangelical and apostolic Scripture requires regeneration of whoever among us wishes to be saved. . . . Wherefore, man not yet regenerate has no free will for good, no strength to perform what is good.[7]

While this may sound pessimistic, the confession continues in a subsequent paragraph:

That the regenerate, in choosing and doing good, work not only passively but actively. For they are moved by God that they may do themselves what they do. For Augustine rightly adduces the saying that "God is said to be our helper. But no one can be helped unless he does something."[8]

Truth is moved from being an abstract concept to being a personal quality. What is good is a result of faith in the One who is the truth, Jesus Christ. The fourth Historic Principle suggests that, "the great touchstone of truth, [is] its tendency to promote holiness." The word *holiness* is seldom used today. It is a term that may carry many, often negative, overtones. The theological term for becoming holy is sanctification. The Reformed understanding of this process is described in the Westminster Confession of Faith as:

They who are effectually called and regenerated, having a new heart and a new spirit created in them, are further sanctified, really and personally, through the virtue of Christ's death and resurrection, by his Word and Spirit dwelling in them; the dominion of the whole body of sin is destroyed, and the several lusts thereof are more and more weakened and mortified, and they are more and more quickened and strengthened, in all saving graces, to the practice of true holiness, without which no man shall see the Lord.

This sanctification is throughout the whole man, yet imperfect in this life."[9]

The Westminster Larger Catechism offers the following response to the question, "What is sanctification?"

> Sanctification is a work of God's grace, whereby they, whom God hath, before the foundation of the world, chosen to be holy, are, in time, through the powerful operation of his Spirit, applying the death and resurrection of Christ unto them, renewed in their whole man after the image of God; having the seeds of repentance unto life, and all other saving graces, put into their hearts, and those graces so stirred up, increased and strengthened, as they more and more die unto sin, and rise in newness of life.[10]

A more contemporary way of speaking of this process is to use the phrase, "new life" as in the Confession of 1967.

> The new life takes shape in a community in which men know that God loves and accepts them in spite of what they are. They therefore accept themselves and love others, knowing that no man has any ground on which to stand, except God's grace.

> The new life does not release a man from conflict with unbelief, pride, lust, fear. He still has to struggle with disheartening difficulties and problems. Nevertheless, as he matures in love and faithfulness in his life with Christ, he lives in freedom and good cheer, bearing witness on good days and evil days, confident that the new life is pleasing to God and helpful to others.[11]

This practical, day-to-day aspect of the complex concept of truth is revealed in dramatic clarity in three catechisms of the *Book of Confessions*. In the Heidelberg Catechism, the response to question 112, "What is required in the Ninth Commandment?" offers an intensely personal understanding of truth.

> That I do not bear false witness against anyone, twist anyone's words, be a gossip or a slanderer, or condemn anyone lightly without a hearing. Rather I am required to avoid, under penalty of God's wrath, all lying and deceit as the works of the devil himself. In judicial and all other matters I am to *love the truth*, and to speak and confess it honestly. Indeed, insofar as I am able, I am to defend and promote my neighbor's good name.[12]

The Westminster Shorter Catechism, which asks first for the text of a given commandment, then for what the commandment requires, and finally, for what the commandment prohibits, on the Ninth Commandment reads:

> The Ninth Commandment requireth the maintaining and promoting of truth between man and man, and of our own and our neighbor's good name, especially in witness-bearing.

The Ninth Commandment forbiddeth whatsoever is prejudicial to truth or injurious to our own or our neighbor's good name.[13]

These teachings draw concrete connections between what today might be compartmentalized as abstract or intellectual truth and interpersonal truth.

The Westminster Larger Catechism expands on the points made in the Shorter Catechism, and also indicates how the Third, Eighth, and Ninth Commandments bear on an understanding of truth. The exposition of what is required by the Ninth Commandment is thorough, particular, personal, and challenging, particularly when the response is reformatted into its ten clauses.

The duties required in the Ninth Commandment are the following:

- the preserving and promoting of truth between man and man, and the good name of our neighbor, as well as our own;
- appearing and standing for the truth;
- and from the heart, sincerely, freely, clearly, and fully, speaking the truth, and only the truth, in matters of judgment and justice, and in all other things whatsoever;
- having a charitable esteem of our neighbors, loving, desiring, and rejoicing in their good name;
- sorrowing for, and covering of their infirmities; freely acknowledging of their gifts and graces, defending their innocency;
- ready receiving of good report, and unwillingness to admit of an evil report concerning them;
- discouraging talebearers, flatterers, and slanderers;
- having love and care of our own good name, and defending it when need requireth;
- keeping of lawful promises;
- studying and practicing of whatsoever things are true, honest, lovely, and of good report.[14]

The basic terms *truth*, *goodness*, and *holiness* are followed in the fourth Historic Principle with an allusion to Jesus' teaching in Matt. 7:17–18: "Every good tree bears good fruit, but the bad tree bears bad fruit. A good tree cannot bear bad fruit, nor can a bad tree bear good fruit." This saying provides an analogy regarding the challenge of separating what is false from what is true. The test appears simple, but it is important to note that the operative word is "fruit" rather than "results." The point is, then, that long-term consequences are what demonstrate whether or not a person's work (or decisions) are good. The story is told of an old man who was planting a peach tree. A young person scoffed at him, "You don't expect to ever eat from the fruit of that tree, do you?" The planter responded, "No. You see, I've enjoyed peaches all my life from trees I didn't plant. Now it's time to see that someone else can share what I have enjoyed." Some sobering conclusions may be drawn from this analogy. For instance, decisions relating to matters of faith are seldom easy and are rarely self-evident. The challenge of making careful decisions in matters of faith requires major intellectual development and discipline. It requires taking the long view and applying a historical skepticism, reflecting an understanding that hasty decisions seldom produce long-lasting results, particularly when related to complex issues.

The fourth Historic Principle further calls into question decision-making practices that use less than the whole range of human capacities. Goodness requires faithfulness to the redeeming love of God in Jesus Christ. This requires faithfulness to a truth that transcends any ideological "party spirit."[15] Decisions, even those with theological support, fail the test of goodness when the result is loveless, harsh, divisive, or arrogant. The fourth Historic Principle applies the Pauline call to speak the truth in love (Eph. 4:15) as an ethic of community life. This ethic involves both what is done as well as *how* it is done. The fourth Historic Principle adds yet another dimension to the responsibilities of church members.[16] It also provides an attribute for understanding chapter III, "The Church and Its Mission." For example, such concern about manner clarifies G-3.0200, "The Church of Jesus Christ is the provisional demonstration of what God intends for all of humanity." We are, all of us, witnesses for God's good news, both in terms of its truth, and even more in terms of its goodness, or its effect on those to whom we relate. Chapter III provides a comprehensive understanding of mission, which is rooted in Scripture. It gives the sense that the Presbyterian Church, as part of the church of Jesus Christ, has an enormous task beyond what any individual can accomplish. There is a wholeness to the mission that Christ gave to the church that dwarfs personal gifts and private perspectives. Most of the arguments I have heard about mission involve discussions of priority and strategy, and rarely consider the wholeness of the mission Christ has given us as disciples.

G-3.0300 presents the scope of mission as it is understood by Presbyterians. The mission of the church as "Christ's faithful evangelist" is described by three participial phrases, which underscores the point that mission is action.

(1) going into the world, making disciples of all nations, baptizing them in the name of the Father and of the Son and of the Holy Spirit, teaching them to observe all he has commanded;

(2) demonstrating by the love of its members for one another and by the quality of its common life the new reality in Christ; sharing in worship, fellowship, and nurture, practicing a deepened life of prayer and service under the guidance of the Holy Spirit;

(3) participating in God's activity in the world through its life for others by
    (a) healing and reconciling and binding up wounds,
    (b) ministering to the needs of the poor, the sick, the lonely, and the powerless,
    (c) engaging in the struggle to free people from sin, fear, oppression, hunger, and injustice,
    (d) giving itself and its substance to the service of those who suffer,
    (e) sharing with Christ in the establishing of his just, peaceable, and loving rule in the world. (G-3.0300a)

All three of these mission enterprises are understood by Presbyterians to be marks of faithfulness. The list is not in priority order, but in terms of the scope of mission activity. Any argument for one or another of these areas of mission must also bear in mind that all of these are included in the *Book of Order*. Mission understood to be as comprehensive as this may be breathtaking. G-3.0400 continues the description of the church's mission, calling for the church to "risk and trust" as it engages in mission.

There follow four phrases beginning with the words, "new openness" that describe additional marks of faithfulness to the church's mission as a servant community. This principle further calls Christians to bear in mind that the means of fulfilling our mission must be open to the same rigorous scrutiny as are the goals and objectives sought. Presbyterians are reminded by the fourth Historic Principle that the end never justifies the means to gain that end.[17]

The fourth Historic Principle is a humbling principle. It stands as a reminder that whatever is understood as true is always a human understanding or perception of the one who alone is Truth. "The inseparable connection between . . . truth and duty" is another way of expressing the importance of "by their fruits."

Aware of the need for careful discernment, Presbyterians emphasize education as the broadening of one's understanding of God's creation, and thus the world around us. The roots of Presbyterian regard for education are found in John Calvin's understanding of Scripture, in his approach to interpreting Scripture, and in Scripture texts that support his concern.

> Since Christians should make progress as long as they live, it is certain that no one is so knowledgeable that he can do without teaching. Thus docility is no small part of our wisdom.[18]

Some of the Scripture references Calvin cites are Eph. 4:10–13, Isa. 59:21, Phil. 3:15, and Rom. 12:3. Calvin's concern for education is shown in his Ecclesiastical Ordinances of 1541, which required an academy that taught languages and other skills necessary for responsible Scripture study.[19] It is also a foundation for preparation for the offices of elder and deacon as required in G-14.0204.

The interplay between study and service is expressed in the first four questions asked of candidates for ordained office.

> Do you trust in Jesus Christ your Savior, acknowledge him Lord of all and Head of the Church, and through him believe in one God, Father, Son, and Holy Spirit?

> Do you accept the Scriptures of the Old and New Testaments to be, by the Holy Spirit, the unique and authoritative witness to Jesus Christ in the Church universal, and God's Word to you?

> Do you sincerely receive and adopt the essential tenets of the Reformed faith as expressed in the confessions of our church as authentic and reliable expositions of what Scripture leads us to believe and do, and will you be instructed and led by those confessions as you lead the people of God?

Will you fulfill your office in obedience to Jesus Christ, under the authority of Scripture, and be continually guided by our confessions? (G-14.0207a–c and G-14.0405b(1)–(4)[20]

These questions follow the order of G-2.0000, beginning with the basis of Christian faith, then moving to the unique authority of Scripture, and then to the confessions as authoritative expositions of Scripture. The fourth question reinforces the importance of the confessions, as indicated in the third set of questions. A truthful affirmative response commits the ordinand to a life of study rooted in Scripture and these confessions.

I was once called by a church asking whether I could give their adult class a one-hour session on "What Presbyterians Believe." When I quickly answered that I could, the caller reported that I was the seventh minister he had contacted and all the previous ones had indicated that the subject was too complex for a single session. A photocopy of chapter II of the *Book of Order*, "The Church and Its Confessions," provided the participants with a comprehensive overview of what Presbyterians believe, and demonstrated how Presbyterians understand the relationship of the confessions to faith. The contents of the *Book of Confessions* are defined as follows: "In these confessional statements the church declares to its members and to the world who and what it is, what it believes, what it resolves to do" (G-2.0100a). The connection between "what it believes" and "what it resolves to do" reiterates the fourth Historic Principle's advocacy of the "inseparable connection between faith and practice, truth and duty." This connection is also exhibited later in chapter II, in four statements of great themes of the Reformed tradition that follow an account of the central affirmation of the Reformed tradition as "the majesty, holiness, and providence of God who creates, sustains, rules, and redeems the world in the freedom of sovereign righteousness and love" (G-2.0500a).

1. The election of the people of God for service as well as for salvation;

2. Covenant life marked by a disciplined concern for order in the church according to the Word of God;

3. A faithful stewardship that shuns ostentation and seeks proper use of the gifts of God's creation;

4. The recognition of the human tendency to idolatry and tyranny, which calls the people of God to work for the transformation of society by seeking justice and living in obedience to the Word of God. (G-2.0500a)

Each of these makes a direct connection between theological affirmation and practical implication. Reflection on these four implications of the doctrine of God's sovereignty is one of the ways Presbyterians can grow in understanding the meaning of membership in the Presbyterian Church (U.S.A.).

The third ordination question begins with the phrase, "Do you sincerely receive and adopt the essential tenets of the Reformed faith?" which has been the focus of continuing dispute. As recently as 1996, the General Assembly received two overtures[21] proposing different approaches to defining the essential tenets. The response of the General Assembly noted "the pain presently felt in parts of the church over a perceived lack of doctrinal clarity." The comment disapproving the two overtures noted the problems of attempts to define the essential tenets in the past, with reference to the General Assembly (PCUSA) actions of 1926 and 1927.[22] As noted in chapter 2 of this book, decisions regarding what is and is not an "essential tenet" rest with the governing body reviewing the candidate for ordination.[23]

Exploration of the fourth Historic Principle has led us deep into the Presbyterian ethos.[24] What began as an examination of abstract theological concepts has led us to considerable examination of our own faithfulness, as well as challenged us to "go into all the world." The connection between truth and mission is one that often seems on the verge of being lost. Attempts to undo this essential connection are not limited to any particular perspective or group within the church. Rediscovery of the significance of this interconnection has marked periods of vitality in our Presbyterian history, and there are always pockets where this vital nerve of church life continues to flourish.

otes

1. *Book of Confessions*, 3.14.

2. Ibid., 5.018.

3. Ibid., 5.023.

4. Ibid., 5.086.

5. Ibid., 5.124.

6. Ibid., 7.182 and 7.190.

7. Ibid., 5.045.

8. Ibid., 5.048.

9. Ibid., 6.075 and 6.076.

10. Ibid., 7.185. Similar language is used in 7.277 in response to the question of how our Baptism is to be improved ". . . for the mortifying of sin and quickening of grace."

11. Ibid., 9.22–23.

12. Ibid., 4.112; italics added.

13. Ibid., 7.077 and 7.078.

14. Ibid., 7.254. The more comprehensive list of prohibitions is found in 7.255.

15. Such as affected the churches in Corinth and Galatia (1 Cor. 1:12–13 and Gal. 1:6).

16. See chap. 3, pp. 25–27.

17. Emil Brunner, *The Divine Imperative* (Philadelphia: The Westminster Press, 1947). "The will to work says, 'he who wills the ends must will the necessary means.' The will to witness says, 'if an end makes it necessary to use dubious means, then this end ought not to be desired' " (p. 277). Brunner has an extensive discussion of "means and ends," as noted in the index of subjects under "Ends," p. 721.

18. William J. Bouwsma, *John Calvin: A Sixteenth-Century Portrait* (New York: Oxford University Press, 1988), p. 187. A thorough discussion of the role of education in the church, complete with Scripture references may be found in John Calvin, *Institutes of the Christian Religion,* edited by John T. McNeill and translated by Ford Lewis Battles (Philadelphia: The Westminster Press, 1960), IV, 5. These issues are also discussed in Richard Osmer, *A Teachable Spirit* (Louisville: Westminster/John Knox Press, 1990), particularly ch. 7, "The Teaching Office in the Thought and Practice of John Calvin."

19. This is a basis for the language requirements for ordination to the ministry of Word and Sacrament in G-14.0310b(3) and G-14.0310d(1).

20. The wording of the last is slightly different because of the need of G-14.0207c to apply to both elders and deacons.

21. Overtures 96–32 and 96–42. For the text, see *Minutes of the 208th General Assembly* (1996), pp. 699 and 707–708.

22. Ibid., p. 42. They could also have referred to the General Assemblies of 1910, 1916, and 1923. For a discussion of this issue in the twenties, see James H. Smylie, *A Brief History of the Presbyterians* (Louisville: Geneva Press), 1996, pp. 113–115. The relevant part of the report of the Special Commission of 1925 is found in *The Presbyterian Constitution and Digest* (Louisville: Office of the General Assembly, 1963), pp. A328f–A331. The report argues that "essential" was intended to mean "essential to the system of doctrine" (pp. A329–A330).

23. However, there are other standards for ordination not related to doctrine that the *Book of Order* and/or a decision of the General Assembly may require as a condition for ordination with the governing body may not disregard.

24. The term "Presbyterian ethos" comes from the title of a course taught by Jack Rogers, to which he refers in *Presbyterian Creeds* (Louisville: Westminster/John Knox Press, 1991), p. 11.

6

$\mathcal{D}$ealing with Differences and Diversity (G-1.0305)

> Forbearance may be what has helped the two most ancient forms of Christian community—congregations and monasteries—to maintain their precious and precarious unity. It may be that with good care such unity grows supple enough to withstand the demands for strict uniformity that so quickly produce division.[1]

$\mathcal{O}$ne of the gifts of the reunion between the former Presbyterian Church in the United States and the United Presbyterian Church in the United States of America was the inclusion of chapter IV of "Form of Government" in the new *Book of Order* titled, "The Church and Its Unity." This chapter included material from chapters titled, "The Visible Church Catholic" from the *Book of Church Order* (PCUS) and "Of the Church" (UPCUSA). What was new was a section titled, "Diversity and Inclusiveness" (G-4.0400). One possible reason for the addition of this section was Article 8 in the Articles of Agreement, "Racial Ethnic Representation, Participation, and Organizations." As the United States of America enters the twenty-first century, the dilemmas of diversity of viewpoint and unity of faith will continue to demand attention.

How surprising, then, to discover that the fifth Historic Principle provides a basis for dealing with this dilemma of unity and diversity.

> That, while under the conviction of the above principle we think it necessary to make effectual provision that all who are admitted as teachers be sound in the faith, we also believe that there are truths and forms with respect to which men of good characters and principles may differ. And in all these we think it the duty both of private Christians and societies to exercise mutual forbearance toward each other. (G-1.0305)

This principle from 1789 reminds us that diversity has been a factor in the American experience from its earliest days. This principle also reminds us that the matter of diversity has challenged Presbyterians throughout our history.

Diversity has a much longer history within the Christian faith. Walter Brueggemann suggests that "the Old Testament in its theological articulation is characteristically dialectical and dialogical, and not transcendentalist."[2] One could follow the discussion of inter-group relations from "a wandering Amamean was my father" (Deut. 26:5) to the reminders that God "executes justice for the orphan and the widow, and who loves the strangers" (Deut. 10:18), to the post-exilic "purification" by separating men from foreign wives (Ezra 10:9–15). Jesus uses the dilemma of diversity when he engages the woman of Samaria at a well (John 4:7ff.) and proposes that a Samaritan is a model neighbor (Luke 10:29–37). The early church struggled with whether a mission to the Gentiles was legitimate (Acts 15). It has been suggested that the doctrine of the Trinity itself "is a symbol of a community that holds together by containing diversity within itself."[3]

The fifth Historic Principle cautions us that the previous two principles describe church life in relationship to church officers who might be misunderstood as authorizing strict doctrinal conformity. With the introductory clause, "while under the conviction of the above principle we think it necessary to make effectual provision that all who are admitted as teachers be sound in the faith," G-1.0305 modifies the two preceding principles by once again issuing a reminder that the historic principles are designed to establish a context for life in the church in which complementary values held in tension.

The main clause of the fifth Historic Principle is the following: "We also believe that there are truths and forms, with respect to which men of good characters and principles may differ." The scope that this clause addresses is "truths and forms," which includes personal opinions and convictions regarding the Christian faith as well as regarding how we go about living as followers of Jesus Christ. This principle notes the diversity in doctrine as well as in practice that has characterized our denomination from its early days. Confessional subscription does not imply a narrow doctrinal uniformity.

It was the morning of November 19, 1729, when the two-year old synod agreed "after long debating upon it" to a lengthy statement regarding what was called "the Affair of the Confession." After noting the importance of freedom of conscience, the action of synod was the following:

> That all the Ministers of this Synod, or that shall hereafter be admitted into this Synod, shall declare their agreement in and approbation of the Confession of Faith with the larger and shorter Catechisms of the Divines at Westminster, as being in all the essential and necessary Articles, good Forms of sound words and systems of Christian Doctrine; and do also adopt the said Confession and Catechisms as the Confession of Faith.

The statement continued, indicating that every presbytery was responsible for upholding this standard.

> And in Case any Minister of this Synod or any Candidate for the Ministry shall have any Scruple with respect to any Article or Articles of said Confession or Catechisms, he shall at the Time of making said Declaration declare his Sentiments to the Presbytery or Synod, who shall notwithstanding admit him to the Exercise of the Ministry within our Bounds to the Ministerial Communion if the Synod or

Presbytery shall judge his scruple or mistake to be only about articles not Essential and necessary in Doctrine, Worship or Government.[4]

The minutes show that immediately following the approval, all ministers but one declared their scruples and were then admitted. What happened that morning in Philadelphia is the precedent for the fifth Historic Principle. American Presbyterians responded to diversity of theological views by developing and adopting a collection of doctrinal statements that were each called a Book of Confessions.[5]

The Confession of 1967 explicitly deals with issues related to diversity of understanding in theology. With characteristic Presbyterian directness, C-67, as it is known, made explicit the situation in which the church in the 1960s found itself. The confession begins by setting forth the basic understanding of the confessional task: "In every age the church has expressed its witness in words and deeds as the need of the time required,"[6] thereby eclipsing the Presbyterian tradition that the Westminster Confession and Catechisms were the "system of doctrine contained in Holy Scripture."

The confession continues, outlining a revised understanding of the role of confessional documents.

Confessions and declarations are subordinate standards in the church, subject to the authority of Jesus Christ, the Word of God, as the Scriptures bear witness to him. No one type of confession is exclusively valid, no one statement is irreformable. Obedience to Jesus Christ alone identifies the one universal church and supplies the continuity of its tradition. This obedience is the ground of the church's duty and freedom to reform itself in life and doctrine as new occasions, in God's providence, may demand.[7]

While this understanding led to controversy until C-67 was adopted, it can be argued that the Westminster Confession itself supports the position outlined in C-67 in its own chapters on "Of the Holy Scripture"[8] and "Of Synods and Councils."[9]

The awareness of diversity is not unique to the American experience. Perhaps the classic instance of diversity of views is found in the discussion between Peter and Paul regarding how a Gentile would become a follower of Jesus Christ. Paul and Barnabas were preaching to the Gentiles but encountered opposition regarding their practice. The result was the so-called Council of Jerusalem, at which a resolution of the dispute was reached and communicated by letter.[10] This account describes an instance where persons of good character upheld opposing points of view with vigor and determination.

When it addresses a Presbyterian understanding of the importance of interpretation of Scripture, C-67 provides a theological position that draws on situations such as that of Peter and Paul in Jerusalem.

> The Bible is to be interpreted in the light of its witness to God's work of reconciliation in Christ. The Scriptures, given under the guidance of the Holy Spirit, are nevertheless the words of men, conditioned by the language, thought forms, and literary fashions of the places and times at which they were written. They reflect views of life, history, and the cosmos which were then current. The church, therefore, has an obligation to approach the Scriptures with literary and historical understanding. As God has spoken his word in diverse cultural situations, the church is confident that he will continue to speak through the Scriptures in a changing world and in every form of human culture.[11]

This statement explicitly recognizes diverse cultural situations as relevant to the changing nature of living as disciples of Jesus Christ.

The age in which we live is characterized by many forms of diversity beyond what our predecessors could have imagined. Awareness of increasing diversity as noted in C-67 has gone well beyond the doctrinal diversity that was the original concern of the fifth Historic Principle to the cultural diversity of our church as well as of our nation.[12] Presbyterian presence has expanded considerably. In the minutes of the first General Assembly in 1789, there were 177 ministers, 111 candidates for ministry, 215 congregations with pastors, and 205 congregations without pastors, a total of 440 congregations.[13] In 1997, there were 14,271 ministers active ministers and 11,295 congregations.[14] Another factor is the changing makeup of Presbyterian churches. The fifteen largest churches (membership from 3,743 to 11,674) account for 2.86 percent of the membership, yet are only .29 percent of the congregations.[15]

> 65.8% of PCUSA congregations have fewer than 200 members. This means that at least two-thirds of the congregations classify as small-membership churches (fewer than 100 in average worship attendance.)[16]

Some other specific concerns pertaining to diversity are related to issues of gender, race, and ethnicity. The inclusion of women as church officers has been a relatively recent phenomenon. The United Presbyterian Church of North America authorized the ordination of women as deacons in 1906. The dates for inclusion of women as officers in the PCUSA were the following: deacons, 1922; elders, 1930; ministers, 1956. In the PCUSA, women were admitted to all offices in 1964.[17] Table 2 indicates how genders compared in 1996 in four categories of service. These data suggest how the historical process has affected the ease of entry into the three offices that the *Book of Order* indicates are open to both men and women.[18]

TABLE 2. COMPARATIVE GENDER DISTRIBUTION BY CATEGORY (1997)

Category	Male	Female	Difference
Member	40.9%	59.1%	18.2%
Deacon	32.9%	67.1%	34.2%
Elders	53.0%	47.0%	-6.0%
Minister of Word & Sacrament	83.8%	16.2%	-67.6%

The racial-ethnic percentage of the total membership of the Presbyterian Church (U.S.A.) in 1996 was 6.8 percent. Table 3 displays the percentages by racial-ethnic description as reported to the denomination.

TABLE 3. RACIAL-ETHNIC DISTRIBUTION OF PRESBYTERIAN MEMBERSHIP (1997)[19]

Race/Ethnicity	Percentage
White	93.2%
Black	2.7%
Asian	2.0%
Hispanic	0.9%
Native American	0.4%
Other	1.1%

The 208th General Assembly, when it resolved to "affirm the goal of increasing the racial ethnic membership to 10 percent of the [PCUSA] membership by the year 2005 and to 20 percent by the year 2010" showed that it was taking seriously the implications of the call to diversity and inclusiveness found in G-4.0400.[20]

> The church in its witness to the uniqueness of the Christian faith is called to mission and must be responsive to diversity in both the church and the world. Thus the fellowship of Christians as it gathers for worship and orders its corporate life will display a rich variety of form, practice, language, program, nurture, and service to suit culture and need. (G-4.0401)

Note that this provision explicitly names gathering for worship and ordering of corporate life in its call to "display a rich variety of form, practice, language, program, nurture, and service to suit culture and need." Diversity, therefore, applies not only to matters of faith and church composition, but also to how the church goes about its work and worship. While the *Book of Order* sometimes appears to set restrictive limits, churches and governing bodies in regions throughout the United States reveal that there are manifold ways of being faithful to Presbyterian polity.

Each session and presbytery may have its own way of going about fulfilling the responsibilities outlined in G-11.0103. This is often evidenced in bylaws and/or operating manuals. The designation of "specified structures" in G-9.0902 intentionally provides for different structural configurations in order to fulfill constitutional requirements. Frequency of meetings also varies considerably.[21] Different ways of going about business during these meetings is often striking. This frequently depends on the number of presbyters attending. This diversity is equally present in meetings of sessions and synods.

G-4.0400 continues:

> Our unity in Christ enables and requires the church to be open to all persons and to the varieties of talents and gifts of God's people, including those who are in the communities of the arts and sciences. (G-4.0402)

This description of openness echoes the call in G-3.0401b with the more daring assertion that it is our unity in Christ that not only enables but *requires* such openness. The next phrase acknowledges the importance of the academic community for the ongoing life of a Presbyterian denomination (this is perhaps a reflection of the interest in academics of a member of the committee to draft the *Book of Order* for the reunited church).

The final paragraph in this section highlights the dilemma of the fifth Historic Principle by juxtaposing two contemporary terms: diversity and inclusiveness. It is a reminder that diversity alone is insufficient.

> The Presbyterian Church (U.S.A.) shall give full expression to the rich diversity within its membership and shall provide means which will assure a greater inclusiveness leading to wholeness in its emerging life. Persons of all racial ethnic groups, different ages, both sexes, various disabilities, diverse geographical areas, different theological positions consistent with the Reformed tradition, as well as different marital conditions (married, single, widowed, or divorced) shall be guaranteed full participation and access to representation in the decision making of the church. (G-9.0104ff.; G-4.0403)

The phrase "full expression" gains meaning in the light of the process begun by the resolution of the 208th General Assembly (1996) to increase ethnic diversity. Full expression involves "full participation and access to representation in the decision making of the church." Diversity by itself would be a hollow goal if there were neither full participation nor access to representation in the decision making of the church. Those explicitly identified as persons whose presence in decision making is required have become known as "protected categories." The categories, as listed below, may seem sociological:

> all racial-ethnic groups
>
> different ages
>
> both sexes
>
> various disabilities
>
> diverse geographical areas
>
> different theological positions consistent with the Reformed tradition
>
> different marital conditions (married, single, widowed, or divorced)

It might be asked, "Why these specific categories? Isn't this allowing our culture to intrude into the church?" Paul's counsel to the Galatians sets a precedent for using sociological categories.

> As many of you as were baptized into Christ have clothed yourselves with Christ. There is no longer Jew or Greek, there is no longer slave or free, there is no longer male and female; for all of you are one in Christ Jesus (Gal. 3:27–28).[22]

The Confession of 1967 offers an interpretation of this teaching from Paul.

> God has created the peoples of the earth to be one universal family. In his reconciling love, he overcomes the barriers between brothers and breaks down every form of discrimination based on racial or ethnic difference, real or imaginary. The church is called to bring all men to receive and uphold one another as persons in all relationships of life: in employment, housing, education, leisure, marriage, family, church, and the exercise of political rights. Therefore, the church labors for the abolition of all racial discrimination and ministers to those injured by it. Congregations, individuals, or groups of Christians who exclude, dominate, or patronize their fellowmen, however subtly, resist the Spirit of God and bring contempt on the faith which they profess.[23]

The Task Force on Theological Pluralism within the Presbyterian Community of Faith, in their report to the 200th General Assembly, "Is Christ Divided?" provided a careful analysis of diversity as it relates to faith.[24]

> Neither diversity nor unity can be given the status of an ideology within the church. Neither can be promoted or enforced by resorting to compulsion. Unity and diversity are inseparable realities. *Unity* is found in God's gift of new life in the Spirit given in and through Jesus Christ. *Diversity* is found in human experiences and expressions of that unifying reality. The existence of Christian community guarantees that faith in the one Jesus Christ will be diverse and that expressions of that faith (theology) will be even more diverse. Yet, because it is faith in Jesus Christ, it is guaranteed that diverse experiences and expressions will be of common faith.[25]

This paragraph succinctly presents the dilemma that arises as the twin factors of diversity and unity are faced, while noting the danger of disturbing the delicate balance between these two realities of our life together.

If these were the only references to the need for inclusiveness and diversity, there would be serious inconsistency between our principles and our practice. However G-4.0403 has an important parenthesis, directing the reader to G-9.0104, where the responsibility for fulfilling the goals of both diversity and inclusiveness is clearly assigned to the governing bodies of the church.[26]

> Governing bodies of the church shall be responsible for implementing the church's commitment to inclusiveness and participation as stated in G-4.0403. All governing bodies shall work to become more open and inclusive and shall pursue affirmative action hiring procedures aiming at correcting patterns of discrimination on the basis of the categories listed in G-4.0403. (G-9.0104a)

> In implementing this commitment, consideration should be given to the gifts and requirements for ministry (G-6.0106) in persons elected or appointed to particular offices or tasks, and to the right of the people to elect their officers. (G-6.0107; G-9.0104b.)

This provision was new at reunion in 1983. Fifteen years later, the implications have yet to be fully realized. The two references to G-6.0100 remind us that while the implementation of diversity is an important commitment, it must be balanced with concern for the gifts and requirements for ministry, as well as the right of the people to elect their officers.

The specific instrument by which compliance with the efforts to fulfill this goal is ensured is the *committee on representation*.

> Each governing body above the session shall elect a committee on representation, whose membership shall consist of equal numbers of men and women. A majority of the members shall be selected from the racial ethnic groups (such as Presbyterians of African, Hispanic, and Asian descent and Native Americans) within the governing body, and the total membership shall include persons from each of the following categories:
>
> 1. majority male membership
> 2. majority female membership
> 3. racial ethnic male membership
> 4. racial ethnic female membership
> 5. youth male and female membership
> 6. persons with disabilities (G-9.0105a)

This committee has been carefully conceived to ensure that it fulfills its purpose. Immediately after reunion, the General Assembly, on the advice of the Advisory Committee on the Constitution, ruled that "the committee cannot be combined with another committee or made a subcommittee. The committee must stand alone."[27]

Four specific functions are assigned to this committee.

- advise the governing bodies with respect to their membership and to that of their committees, boards, agencies, and other units in implementing the principles of participation and inclusiveness to ensure fair and effective representation in the decision making of the church. (G-9.0105b).
- serve both as an advocate for the representation of racial ethnic members, women, different age groups, and persons with disabilities, and as a continuing resource to the particular governing body in these areas . . . and report annually . . . (G-9.0105c).
- prior to nomination or appointment of racial ethnic members to committees, boards, agencies, or other units, the committee on representation shall consult with the appropriate racial ethnic membership through a person or persons designated by that racial ethnic membership . . . (G-9.0105d).
- advise the governing body on the employment of personnel, in accordance with the principles of participation and representation (G-4.0403), and in conformity with a churchwide plan for equal employment opportunity. (G-13.0201b; G-9.0105e).

Making this committee effective in its work is an important assignment for every officer and member of the Presbyterian church. While this process has contributed to our life together, there is still much work remaining in this area.

Notice that G-9.0105a required committees on representation for each governing body above the session. A question may arise as to whether the session is exempt from concern for inclusiveness. The response to this question is found in chapter X in "Form of Government," in a statement regarding the minutes of session.

The minutes shall state the composition of the session with regard to racial ethnic members, women, men, age groups, and persons with disabilities, and how this corresponds to the composition of the congregation. (G-10.0301)

When this provision is connected with a provision found in the section "Governing Bodies: Principles of Administration" in chapter IX, its force is realized.

At least once a year every governing body above a session shall review the records of the proceedings of the next lower governing body. (G-9.0407c)

The nature of this review is to determine whether:

1. The proceedings have been correctly recorded;
2. The proceedings have been regular and in accordance with the *Constitution*;
3. The proceedings have been prudent and equitable;

4. The proceedings have been faithful to the mission of the whole church;

5. The lawful injunctions of a higher governing body have been obeyed. (G-9.0409a)

While it is a circuitous route to follow, this is how sessions are held responsible for their work in the direction of inclusiveness.[28]

The foregoing discussion of diversity in its various forms unpacks the first sentence of the fifth Historic Principle. The second sentence of the fifth Historic Principle indicates the appropriate attitude for dealing with diversity within the church.

> We think it the duty both of private Christians and societies to exercise mutual forbearance toward each other.

The word *forbearance* is seldom used in modern times. It is a biblical word, particularly evident in the New Testament. Ephesians 4:1–3 clarifies what the drafters of this principle meant by forbearance.

> I therefore, the prisoner in the Lord, beg you to lead a life worthy of the calling to which you have been called, with all humility and gentleness, with patience, bearing with one another in love, making every effort to maintain the unity of the Spirit in the bond of peace.

The fifth Historic Principle reminds us of Paul's teaching about how members of the body of Christ are to treat one another. Paul's exhortation echoes Jesus' instruction in the Golden Rule, that we should do for others what we want them to do for us (Matt. 7:12).

Relationships among Christians has always been a delicate subject. The prayer of Jesus, "That they may all be one" as recorded in John 17:21 hints at the disputes and tensions that characterized the disciples' relationships. The prayer continues in the same verse, "As you, Father, are in me and I am in you, may they also be in us, so that the world may believe that you have sent me." This passage is often cited with regard to ecumenical relations, without recognition of its relevance for how brother and sister Christians within the same tradition treat one another. Also often overlooked is the implication that these relationships should be modeled on the relations among the persons of the Trinity.

This teaching is made more trenchant in the First Epistle of John, which was a response to a community that had a tendency toward rivalry and factions.

> We know that we have passed from death to life because we love one another. . .
>
> We know love by this, that [Christ] laid down his life for us—and we ought to lay down our lives for one another. (1 John 3:14, 16)

Here forbearance becomes self-sacrifice for the sake of a brother or sister. This epistle indicates that there may have been both internal and external pressures on the community of faith to which John writes.

The problem of factionalism was not limited to the Johannine communities. Paul wrote to the church in Corinth, "For it has been reported to me by Chloe's people that there are quarrels among you, my brothers and sisters" (1 Cor. 1:11). Paul deals in this Epistle with various controversies that were dividing people in the Corinthian church. Paul's pleas for peace between the factions take the shape of a theological exposition on the church as the body of Christ. After describing his understanding of this doctrine, Paul writes, "Now you are the body of Christ and individually members of it" (1 Cor. 12:27). The well-known thirteenth chapter of 1 Corinthians regarding the nature of love suggests that Paul's intention was to guide the Corinthians in their understanding of what was involved in being a member, and how that affected their treatment of one another.

A call to forbearance is also found in the instructions in the Epistles of Peter.

> Finally, all of you, have unity of spirit, sympathy, love for one another, a tender heart and a humble mind. Do not repay evil for evil or abuse for abuse; but, on the contrary, repay with a blessing (1 Peter 3:8–9).[29]

Presbyterians need to seek forbearance in dealings with one another if we are to exemplify the quality of life which our Savior would have us live.

It is worth noting that the instruction in the fifth Historic Principle refers not only to those who are members of a particular denomination but also to other groups. The "new openness to God's continuing reformation of the Church ecumenical, that it might be a more effective instrument of mission in the world" delineated in G-3.0401d flows from this principle. Explicit responsibility for such relationships is assigned to sessions (G-10.0102q), to presbyteries (G-11.0103u), to synods (G-12.0102p), and to the General Assembly (G-13.0103u). The commitment to various types of ecumenical enterprises is set forth in G-15.0100, "Ecumenical Commitment." The remainder of chapter XV discusses relations with other denominations (G-15.0200) and church union (G-15.0300). Chapter XVI in "Form of Government" discusses how union churches are established and states general procedures in such cases. Chapter XVII in "Form of Government" provides similar information regarding union governing bodies.

It is evidenced by this stream within the *Book of Order* that "mutual forbearance" with other societies is something to which the Presbyterian Church (U.S.A.) is committed. This ecumenical commitment is longstanding. Sometimes this has meant making efforts to heal divisions within the Presbyterian Church.[30] Sometimes it has been manifested in support for ecumenical organizations, such as the National Council of Churches.[31] In 1960, Eugene Carson Blake, former Stated Clerk of the UPCUSA, initiated a proposal for the formation of The Consultation on Church Union, known as COCU.[32] There have always been numerous Presbyterian leaders in the international ecumenical movement, although that presence has not consistently been appreciated within the church. In 1997, the 209th General Assembly proposed a "Formula of Agreement" involving the Evangelical Lutheran Church, the Presbyterian Church (U.S.A.), the Reformed Church in America, and the United Church of Christ. This relationship was defined as "mutual respect, mutual admonition,"[33] which puts into contemporary language the thrust of "mutual forbearance" from the fifth Historic Principle.

Another contemporary expression of "mutual forbearance" is found in recent calls for civility in our modern life. Civility goes beyond toleration to include mutual agreement to use respectful language with one another, resisting the tendency to use extreme words when discussing differences, and recognition that we all profess to be disciples of one Lord, Jesus Christ. We need to rediscover the adventure and discipline suggested by G-4.0301d: "Presbyters are not simply to reflect the will of the people, but rather to seek together to find and represent the will of Christ."

The following news item provides an example of how the principle of mutual forbearance affects how Presbyterians respond in crisis situations.

> Extreme loyalists set fires in ten Roman Catholic churches throughout Ireland. On learning about the fires, the moderator of the Presbyterian Church in Ireland, Dr. John Dixon, drove straight to St. James Church near Crumlin to view what remained of the church. He was accompanied by Roman Catholic Bishop Patrick Walsh. Great sympathy was expressed.
>
> Then the arguments over the traditional march came forth and more violence ending with the fire bombing which killed three Roman Catholic children. The feelings went from stubborn anger to frustrated sadness.
>
> A top Presbyterian leader said that though the hard-liners in his country could not be reasoned with, he hoped that their excesses would alienate them from the majority of the people of Northern Ireland.
>
> The Presbyterian moderator said ". . . tolerance . . . is essential for the well-being of the community of life. . . . In these tense days . . . let us love not in word only but also in deeds and actions. . . ."[34]

Moderator Dixon's remark offers a contemporary expression of the fifth Historic Principle in action.

otes

1. Kathleen Norris, *Amazing Grace: A Vocabulary of Faith* (New York: Riverhead Books, 1998),p. 158.

2. Walter Brueggemann, *Theology of the Old Testament: Testimony, Dispute, Advocacy* (Minneapolis: Fortress Press, 1977), p. 83.

3. Norris, *Amazing Grace*, p. 289

4. Material regarding this meeting is found in Guy S. Klett, ed., *Minutes of the Presbyterian Church in America: 1706–1788* (Philadelphia: Presbyterian Historical Society, 1976), pp. 103–104. Spelling has been modernized for this presentation, abbreviations have been spelled out, but capitalization is from the original text as printed.

5. See James H. Smylie, *A Brief History of the Presbyterians* (Louisville: Geneva Press, 1996), pp. 132–134 for a brief discussion of the process. A longer treatment may be found in Jack Rogers, *Presbyterian Creeds* (Louisville: Westminster/John Knox Press, 1991), pp. 202–230.

6. *Book of Confessions*, 9.02.

7. Ibid., 9.03. Note how this language has been inserted in G-2.0200. The process for amending the confessional documents is outlined in G-18.0200. Note how this process differs from amending the *Book of Order* (G-18.0300).

8. Ibid., 6.001–010.

9. Ibid., 6.173–175.

10. Acts 14:21–28; Acts 15:1–2, 22–29. The account of the Council in Acts 15 was one basis for Presbyterians establishing their form of church government. The record of the meeting suggests that the dynamics of decision making have not changed much since that meeting.

11. *Book of Confessions*, 9.29.

12. IBM had an advertising campaign with the motto, "diversity works." Under a full-page, full-color picture of a microchip with this phrase in the middle, there is the line: "IBM. Powered by people as diverse as the marketplace we serve" *Atlantic Monthly* (August 1998), p. 46.

13. James H. Smylie, *A Brief History of the Presbyterians* (Louisville: Geneva Press, 1996), p. 65. The 49 percent rate of churches without pastors shows the perilous state of the church in those times.

14. *Comparative Statistics: 1997* (Louisville: Research Services, a Ministry of the General Assembly Council, Congregational Ministries Division, 1998), pp. 2, 12. This annual publication by Research Services is available from Presbyterian Distribution Service for $5. There were 6,587 retired ministers indicated in this report.

15. Ibid., pp. 3, 12. Calculation by the author.

16. Ibid., p. 1.

17. Historical note to G-6.0105, *Book of Order: Annotated Edition* (Louisville: Office of the General Assembly, 1998).

18. *Book of Order*, G-6.0105. Data from *Comparative Statistics*, p. 27.

19. *Comparative Statistics*, p. 27.

20. *Minutes of the 208th General Assembly* (1996), p. 378, 33.148.

21. See G-11.0201.

22. Similar passages are 1 Cor. 12:13 and Col. 3:11.

23. *Book of Confessions*, 9.45.

24. *Minutes of the 200th General Assembly* (1988), pp. 826–851.

25. Ibid., pp. 57, 174, and 842; italics added.

26. *Governing bodies* are session, presbytery, synod, and General Assembly (G-9.0101). Some guidance is offered for approaching this task.

27. *Minutes of the 196th General Assembly* (1986), p. 605, 55.108.

28. Explicit responsibilities are delineated in G-11.0302; 12.0301; 13.0108; 13.0202b; 14.0201d; and 14.0513f.

29. Cited in the Westminster Larger Catechism, *Book of Confessions*, 7.245. The reference supports part of the answer to the question, "What are the duties required in the Sixth Commandment?

30. Smylie, *A Brief History of the Presbyterians*, p. 86, provides a chart of the various "Presbyterian Family Connections" in the United States of America.

31. Ibid., p. 107. The original name was the Federal Council of Churches when it was founded in 1908.

32. Ibid., p. 137.

33. This phrase now appears in G-15.0302d, taken from "A Formula of Agreement." The proposal is found in *Minutes of the 209th General Assembly* (1997), 11.0089, p. 115.

34. "Mission News by Marj [Carpenter]," item no. 801, e-mail item written Saturday, July 25, 1998, at 11:50 a.m.

7

ho Chooses Whom and Why (G-1.0306)

Standing with One Another: Solidarity Across Difference[1]

A conversation between an eminent Methodist seminary professor and a Presbyterian college professor hit a snag at the mention of the word *bishop*. The Methodist seminary professor reflected a moment and then commented, "Oh, I had forgotten about the Presbyterian irrational hatred of bishops." The intensity of this comment suggests how important the various types of polity are to Protestants.

There are three families of Christian polity: congregational, episcopal, and presbyterian. The *congregational* form emphasizes the local church as the key unit of governance. Each congregation elects its own officers and develops its own rules, bylaws, and procedures. A congregation may affiliate with a denomination for certain limited purposes, and may send delegates to meetings of groupings in larger geographical areas, understanding that each church reserves the right to determine for itself whether to follow the decisions of the larger body. Within congregational polity, local churches have equal voice in decision-making procedures. Denomination is, therefore, understood in terms of a partnership or consortium that may be exited by vote of the local congregation. This is a pure democracy. While a church board may oversee church operations, no decision is final until the congregation votes on the matter.

Episcopal polity derives its appellation from a Greek word for "overseer" or "watcher." In Greek civil government, the term designated officials at various levels. In Judaism, the title was also used for overseers in various ways. While the term is used in the New Testament,[2] it developed ecclesiastical usage in subsequent years.

Churches with episcopal polity (such as Roman Catholic, Episcopal, and Methodist) have bishops who are in charge of areas of authority. Ordination as a bishop is often considered a separate rite or sacrament beyond the ordination of priests, which is itself understood, by some churches with this type of polity, as a continuation of an unbroken tradition begun with Jesus ordaining the original twelve disciples. Bishops appoint priests to positions in local churches. Consultation with the local parish in this process varies from none at all to major consultation. Doctrine and policy tend to flow down from bishops to local churches. While the people of the church may form councils or other boards, there is emphasis on uniformity of worship and practice.

Presbyterian polity is derived from the Greek word meaning "elder." The original concept comes from a Hebrew root, זקן (zqn), meaning "one who wears a beard."[3] The term is used extensively in Exodus, beginning in Ex. 3:18. There are numerous instances of the corresponding Greek word in the New Testament. Usage in the Gospels refers to Jewish authorities. There are thirteen references in Acts, beginning with Acts 11:30. There are five instances in Acts 15 (the Council of Jerusalem), where the formula is "the apostles and the elders." The other major references are in 1 Tim. 5:1, 17, 19, and Titus 1:7, where the terms *bishop* and *elder* both appear. The hallmark of churches using the Presbyterian system is the use of elders in governance in sessions or consistories in local churches. The Presbyterian system is considered an intermediate form of church government between the congregational and episcopal forms. The issue raised by a comparison of forms of polity can be stated as follows: Who gets to decide which issues?

A recent instance where the difference between systems of polity become an issue illustrates the depth of commitment to Presbyterian government. In 1996, the 209th General Assembly sent several overtures regarding changes to the *Book of Order* proposed by the Special Committee on the Consultation on Church Union for vote by the presbyteries. Some of these changes would have added "bishop" to the offices of ministry.[4] The vote of the presbyteries on this proposal was 66 in favor, 104 opposed, and 2 "no action."[5] Concern regarding the *role* of bishops was generally regarded as a major factor leading to the negative vote.

The sixth Historic Principle states:

> That though the character, qualifications, and authority of Church officers are laid down in the Holy Scriptures, as well as the proper method of their investiture and institution, yet the election of the persons to the exercise of this authority, in any particular society, is in that society. (G-1.0306)

This principle describes what may appear to be in conflict with the third Historic Principle (G-1.0303), which discusses the qualifications for church office. The word *yet*, however, indicates that the two principles need one another. The reference to "any particular society" intentionally enables broad application of this principle in the life of the local church, as well as in the governing bodies of the church.

The sixth Historic Principle reflects the historic Reformed dread of bishops, which is clearly evidenced in the work of John Calvin. Calvin frames the issue as he presents his case in the *Institutes of the Christian Religion*.

> Someone now asks whether the minister ought to be chosen by the whole church, or only by his colleagues and the elders charged with the censure of morals, or whether he ought to be appointed by the authority of a single person.[6]

John T. McNeill, who edited the Library of Christian Classics edition of *The Institutes*, comments on this passage that "Calvin habitually expresses a preference for plural authority rather than that of individuals."[7] Calvin cites Titus 1:5, 1 Tim. 5:22, and Acts 14:23 in support of his contention that "the people" should elect their ministers. Calvin apparently relies on the Greek word Χειροτονεω (*keirotoneo*), meaning "to elect by a show of hands."[8] He also cites Cyprian, the early church father who drew on Lev. 8:4–6, Num. 20:25–27, Acts 1:15ff., and Acts 6:2–7 in support of election by the congregation.[9] Calvin concludes:

> We therefore hold that this call of a minister is lawful according to the Word of God when those who seemed fit are created by the consent and approval of the people.[10]

The writings of Calvin thus support election of pastors by the people served rather than by a process of appointment by one individual or even a group of individuals.

The *Book of Confessions* displays the Reformed antipathy toward bishops. The Scots Confession uses the term only when it refers to Jesus Christ as one appointed by God, "to be our head, our brother, our pastor, and the great bishop of our souls."[11] The Second Helvetic Confession indicates that reference to Christ as "bishop" is understood as reference to a pastoral office.

> For we teach that Christ the Lord is, and remains the only universal pastor, the highest Pontiff before God the Father; and that in the Church he himself performs all the duties of a bishop or pastor, even to the world's end.[12]

There are also instances of anti-episcopal sentiment in the Second Helvetic Confession.[13] Thus antipathy toward bishops as a threat to the rights of the people is deeply rooted in the Presbyterian tradition.

The *Book of Order* provides another theological foundation for this attitude in chapter II of "Form of Government: The Church and Its Confessions," in the context of God's sovereignty.

> The recognition of the human tendency to idolatry and tyranny, which calls the people of God to work for the transformation of society by seeking justice and living in obedience to the Word of God. (G-2.0500a(4))

The Presbyterian heritage from Scotland imprinted a concern about "the human tendency to idolatry and tyranny," the solution for which was broad-based decision making. The Presbyterian reputation for committees is rooted in this understanding. Providing every member with the authority to join with the others in determining their leaders was considered a hedge against the tendency to tyranny, as well as an embodiment of our commitment to seek justice. Unfortunately, this insight seems to have been lost for many Presbyterians today.

The sixth Historic Principle is reaffirmed within chapter VI of "Form of Government: The Church and Its Officers," with some language that might lead to confusion or misunderstanding if it is not read carefully or cited in its entirety.

> The government of this church is representative, and the right of God's people to elect their officers is inalienable. Therefore, no person can be placed in any permanent office in a congregation or governing body of the church except by election of that body. (G-6.0107)

The first sentence adds two key words for understanding how the sixth Historic Principle works in the *Book of Order.* The first is "representative." Government is through groups elected by the people, rather than directly by the people.[14] This is referred to as a representative democracy or a republic, which is the form in government of the United States of America.

The second key word is "inalienable," a word found in the Declaration of Independence. This strong word indicates that this right is one that cannot be given up, transferred, or surrendered.[15] What cannot be given up is the right of the people to elect persons to permanent office. These offices are pastor, elder, and deacon in the congregation, and moderator and clerk in a governing body. This provision was tested in a case decided by the General Assembly Permanent Judicial Commission on June 18, 1984, regarding the Westminster Presbyterian Church of Buffalo, NY. Citing this provision of the *Book of Order,* the opinion reads:

> Argument has been made that each congregation has constitutional power and authority in the selection of its own officers for ordination. That authority can be exercised only within the constitutional framework of the larger church to which each member church is connected.[16]

The right to elect is inalienable but not unlimited. It is a right that must be exercised within the bounds of the polity of the denomination. Of the five items of business on which a congregation may vote,[17] four are related to the implementation of the sixth Historic Principle. These relate directly to the choice of who will "bear rule" in the governance of the congregation. It is seldom understood that the right of members to vote for officers in the congregation is a privilege Presbyterians have defended for centuries.

The provisions found in G-14.0200, "Electing and Ordaining Elders and Deacons," demonstrate another way in which the sixth Historic Principle impacts the life of the church. The nominating committee for a congregation is constituted in such a way that:

> Other members of the committee, in sufficient number to constitute a majority thereof (exclusive of the pastor), shall be chosen by the congregation or by such organizations within the church as the congregation may designate, none of whom

may be in active service on the session or in active service on the board of deacons. (G-14.0201b)

While this may seem a cumbersome way of describing how a nominating committee is developed, it ensures that the people of the congregation always constitute a majority and that the makeup reflects the choice of the people.

There are three subsequent paragraphs regarding nominations for office in the congregation. These have to do with special provisions for small churches (G-14.0201c and G-14.0202a(3)), a reminder of the need for "participation and representation" (G-14.0201d and G-14.0202a(1) and (2)), and assurance that opportunity for nominations from the floor are provided (G-14.0201e). This last provision further underscores the concern that the people will have the opportunity to express their will.

G-14.0502 outlines the process for the congregation calling a permanent pastor.[18] "The right of the people" is evident in this three-paragraph description of a process that often takes as long as eighteen months. For example, the composition of the pastor nominating committee is restricted only by the phrase, "which shall be representative of the whole congregation" (G-14.0502a). The requirement for public notice of the meeting to elect the nominating committee is further evidence that the rights of members of the congregation are intended to be carefully preserved.

Another notable feature is that the session is mentioned only once in these paragraphs that describe the process of calling a pastor. This is in regard to calling a meeting of the congregation to hear and vote on the report of the nominating committee (G-14.0502c). The nominating committee is elected by the congregation and reports to the body that elected it, consistent with the sixth Historic Principle. Other communications with the session for such things as approving the information on a church information form and determining appropriate proposed salary are related to the ongoing work of the session. Any other communication is on the basis of courtesy, rather than requirement, since the nominating committee is the only committee within a congregation not required to report to the session.

There is careful delineation of how the congregational meeting to hear the report of the pastor nominating committee is to be handled (G-14.0503). The moderator first asks the following: "Are you ready to proceed to the election of a pastor (associate pastor)?" Then the question is voiced: "The vote shall be upon the question whether the congregation, under the will of God, shall call the person nominated to be its pastor (associate pastor)." It is also specified that the vote "shall be taken by ballot," indicating that written ballots are to be used. There is a provision for dissent.

> If it appears that a substantial minority of the voters are averse to the nominee who has received a majority of the votes, and that they cannot be persuaded to concur in the call, the moderator shall recommend to the majority that they not prosecute the call. (G-14.0505).

These provisions are designed to ensure that the vote of the people of the church is protected from interference from some other quarter, and to indicate that the person called becomes the pastor of all the people, including those who do not vote for that person. Presbyteries sometimes set percentage limits regarding the level of dissent beyond which the presbytery will not approve a call.

It is emphasized that a nominating committee is required to keep in touch with the committee on ministry of the presbytery. Usually this is accomplished through a liaison appointed by the committee who works with the nominating committee throughout their search. Since ministers are members of a presbytery, "No minister or candidate shall receive a call except through the hands of his or her own presbytery" (G-14.0507b).

An often-repeated complaint is about how long it takes a church to call a new pastor. While many reasons have been put forward to account for the delay, there are some reasons why the process is complex. One is that the committee usually has minimal background and needs time to learn their assignment. Another is that every committee's search is nationwide, at least in principle,[19] so it takes time and work to prepare appropriate documents to participate in a process of this scope. The search is limited, in that neither an associate pastor (G-14.0501f), nor an interim pastor (G-14.0513b, last sentence) may be called as the next installed pastor. The rationale for these prohibitions is past experience where such cases have proved unfortunate, and also to remove the temptation of someone already in a position within the congregation to seek the position of pastor.

Another complicating factor is that a "call" of a Presbyterian church to a pastor is a three-part contract involving the church, the pastor, and the presbytery as equal parties. While it is the congregation that provides the financial support of the pastor in most cases,[20] Presbyterians are also committed to the "freedom of the pulpit."[21] Presbytery supervision of ministers of the Word and Sacrament provides the balance to ensure that freedom of the pulpit does not become simply an endorsement of individualism. This three-part arrangement allows for the possibility of mediation should troubles emerge in the life of a congregation (G-11.0502). Awareness that the presbytery is a partner in the call of a pastor challenges the unfortunate, yet often-expressed feeling that presbytery is an "outsider" rather than a major partner. The final expression of this significant partnership is found in G-14.0600, "Dissolution of Pastoral Relationships": "The pastoral relationship between a pastor, associate pastor, or assistant pastor and a church may be dissolved only by presbytery" (G-14.0601). The Presbyterian system of government draws its strength from the balancing of different perspectives.

The sixth Historic Principle is also at work in elections for offices other than those that are permanent, namely, moderators and clerks,[22] although with some modification. A moderator or clerk must be eligible for membership in the body electing the officer. *Eligibility* means ordination as a presbyter, although an elder need not currently be serving on session to be elected clerk of session.[23] Although there is no provision for a moderator of the session when there is no installed pastor in G-9.0201, the situation is remedied in G-10.0103b, where it indicates that the presbytery may appoint a moderator. There is a subtle, yet significant distinction between an installed pastor and an appointed moderator.

> The session of a particular church consists of the pastor or co-pastors, the associate pastors, and the elders in active service. *All members of the session*, including the pastor, co-pastors, and associate pastors, are *entitled* to vote. (G-10.0101; italics added)

An appointed moderator of a session is excluded from voting in session meetings. The basis for this exclusion is that the moderator has been appointed by the presbytery, not elected, as is the pastor, by the congregation. While this may appear to be a minor point, it indicates how seriously the sixth Historic Principle is taken in determining relationships within the church.

"Society" in the sixth Historic Principle is inclusive, even if it is a limited franchise. We will explore in the next chapter the concept of "designated authority," which provides an additional dimension of understanding how and why Presbyterians determine which body makes which decisions. There is an understandable tendency to want to be directly involved in all decisions that affect us, yet we live in a republic where those whom we elect make all sorts of decisions for us. Town council members, school board members, representatives, senators, and boards of director make decisions for us daily. It is curious that what is accepted in public life is questioned when it comes to church life!

Unfortunately, cynicism about voting for civil government may have infected participation in election within nongovernmental entities, including the church. What the *Book of Order* declares as an "inalienable right" of church government is often not exercised. We are often poor stewards of this inalienable right. There may also a tendency toward the attitude displayed on bumper stickers that read, "Don't blame me—I didn't vote for _____." This seemingly bold proclamation may, in fact, indicate irresponsibility, particularly if it indicates that the owner of the vehicle didn't vote at all. When Presbyterians, for whatever reason, decide that it is easier to avoid a vote than to make one, they relinquish a right and a privilege of being part of the community of faith.

The Presbyterian system of church order calls for disciplined and responsible participation by members of the church. The sixth Historic Principle inserts the democratic, broad-based assent of the members into the ongoing leadership of the church. The broader the base, the better the decision. That this is a representative democratic system means that not every decision is put to a vote of the people. While it may seem that one voice or one vote is not worth the effort, Presbyterian history shows that it is sometimes the one voice raised in comment or question that determines the outcome of a vote.

Presbyterians are convinced that God's Spirit can speak through an individual seeking to serve our Lord.

otes

1. Title of Alumni/ae Weekend, April 23–24, 1999, announced in *Union News* (New York: Union Theological Seminary, 1999).

2. Acts 20:28, Phil. 1:1, 1 Tim. 3:2, Titus 1:7, and 1 Peter 2:25.

3. Gerhard Friedrich, *Theological Dictionary of the New Testament*, vol. VI (Grand Rapids: Wm. B. Eerdmans Publishing Co., 1968), p. 655, ftn. 20.

4. *Minutes of the 209th General Assembly* (1996), 16.075, pp. 215–218. A comment found on p. 209, par. 16.030, requested COCU to adopt the terminology of "representative bishop."

5. *Minutes of the 210th General Assembly* (1997), 12.0117, p. 133.

6. John Calvin, *Institutes of the Christian Religion*, edited by John T. McNeill and translated by Ford Lewis Battles (Philadelphia: The Westminster Press, 1960), IV.III.15, p. 1065.

7. Ibid., p. 1065, ftn. 13.

8. Ibid., p. 1066, ftn. 14.

9. Ibid., ftn. 15.

10. Ibid., p. 1066.

11. *Book of Confessions*, 3.08. The phrasing is from 1 Peter 2:25.

12. Ibid., 5.131. Note also 5.160 where ministers are given this title.

13. See *Book of Confessions*, 5.014, 5.135, and 5.162.

14. Direct government by the people is pure democracy.

15. *Webster's New Collegiate Dictionary* (Springfield, MA: G & C Merriam Company, 1980), p. 574.

16. *Union Presbyterian Church of Blasdell vs. The Presbytery of Western New York*, in *Minutes of the 197th General Assembly* (1985), p. 120.

17. Chapter VII in "Form of Government: The Particular Church," section G-7.0300, "Meetings of the Congregation," particularly G-7.0304a (1), (2), (3), and (5).

18. "Permanent pastor" refers to those positions described in G-14.0501.

19. The number of active ministers in PCUSA in 1996 was 14,384. See *Comparative Statistics: 1997* (Louisville: Research Services, a Ministry of the General Assembly Council, Congregational Ministries Division, 1998), table 7, p. 12. Not all ministers are considered actively seeking, indicating those who are interested in another call.

20. Some churches in special circumstances receive aid from other governing bodies to enable the church to move toward self-supporting status. This is usually a response to specific mission needs of the congregation.

21. See W-1.4005 for the pastor's five responsibilities relating to worship, which demonstrates the limited scope of uniquely pastoral prerogatives in worship. This whole section (W-1.4000) also sets out session responsibilities and how these coordinate with the pastor.

22. The basic description of these officers is found in G-9.0200.

23. See the answer of the Advisory Committee on the Constitution to Communication 4–88 in *Minutes of the 200th General Assembly* (1988), p. 137, par. 12.188–189.

8
${\mathcal{W}}$ho Makes Which Decisions (G-1.0307)?

Power versus Authority

${\mathcal{A}}$t first glance, "power" and "authority" may appear to be synonyms. While the terms are certainly related to each other, understanding how they differ is basic for appreciating the significance of the seventh Historic Principle. Max Weber, the German sociologist who pioneered in the field of sociology of religion, distinguished between "legitimate authority" and "illegitimate authority" as it affected religion, as well as other spheres of human activity.[1]

Sociologist Paul Harrison in his book, *Authority and Power in a Free Church Tradition,* used the word "power" to designate what Weber termed "illegitimate authority."

> Power as it is used here signifies the ability of a person or group to determine the action of others without regard for their needs or desires.[2]

Harrison reserved "authority" to identify what Weber called "legitimate authority: "Authority . . . indicates a right to exercise power."[3] His book offers an analysis of how various figures in the American Baptist Convention used both authority and power in going about their mission.

Harrison suggests that there are three forms of authority: traditional, rational-legal, and charismatic.[4] Traditional authority is based on the traditions of the community. Rational-legal authority confers a legal right based on the official and rational laws of the community. Charismatic authority is based on the personality of the leader who draws the loyalty of people even if they must disregard established traditions and laws.

Ordination is an example of granting a person the right to exercise certain authority. In fact, from Harrison's perspective, the *Book of Order* could be considered a catalog of how the necessary authority is assigned for a church to function. Which of the entities is authorized to decide the issues of church life? What is the scope of authority specific officers have as they fulfill their obligations in the church? And how do individuals go about discharging their responsibilities? The seventh Historic Principle addresses these questions.

> That all Church power, whether exercised by the body in general or in the way of representation by delegated authority, is only ministerial and declarative; that is to

say, that the Holy Scriptures are the only rule of faith and manners; that no Church governing body ought to pretend to make laws to bind the conscience in virtue of their own authority; and that all their decisions should be founded upon the revealed will of God. Now though it will easily be admitted that all synods and councils may err, through the frailty inseparable from humanity, yet there is much greater danger from the usurped claim of making laws than from the right of judging upon laws already made, and common to all who profess the gospel, although this right, as necessity requires in the present state, be lodged with fallible men. (G-1.0307)

The seventh Historic Principle is the longest and most complex of all the historic principles.[5] There are four major points in the first sentence, followed by three phrases in the second sentence. For ease of discussion, this principle will be examined phrase by phrase.

1a. **That all Church power, whether exercised by the body in general or in the way of representation by delegated authority, is only ministerial and declarative.**[6]

"All church power" hearkens back to the first sentence of the *Book of Order*, which indicates that the "power source" for the church is the Lord of the Church, Jesus Christ. Furthermore, "It [church power] belongs to Christ alone to rule, to teach, to call, and to use the Church as he wills, exercising *his authority* by the ministry of women and men for the establishment and extension of his Kingdom" (G-1.0100b; italics added). Church power must be understood and used as a gift from Christ for a specific purpose.

The phrase "ministerial and declarative" describes the nature of church power. *Ministerial* refers to ministers, but in a particular way seldom used in modern discourse. This almost archaic usage is derived from the original sense of "minister" as a servant. According to *The Oxford English Dictionary on Historical Principles*, the first meaning of the term "ministerial" is "pertaining to, or entrusted with, the execution of . . . the commands of a superior."[7] This adjective confirms the notion of church power as a gift. Ministers are thus understood as God's servants, using whatever power they have in the way God in Christ intends such power to be used.

The other defining adjective is "declarative." A declaration makes something clear, ". . . the action of setting forth or announcing openly, explicitly, or formally; positive statement or assertion."[8] The opposite type of sentence is the imperative sentence, used for issuing orders. This adds to the description of church power that Christ's power is given to his servants for the fulfillment of the Great Commission in Matt. 28:18–20. It is the power of witness, suggested in a paraphrase of 2 Cor. 1:4–5: "God helps us in all our troubles, so that we are able to help others using what we have received from God."[9] This clause in the seventh Historic Principle reminds us that we are all witnesses, responsible for telling what we know about God's love in Jesus

Christ. The dependent clause within this first phrase establishes the scope of application of this evangelical principle with the words, "whether exercised by the body in general or in the way of representation by delegated authority." This is a breathtakingly comprehensive phrase that applies the ethic of nonimperative witness to persons and groups equally.

The confessions of the Presbyterian Church (U.S.A.) demonstrate that this concern has an extensive basis, with particular emphasis on church power. There are numerous references in the *Book of Confessions* to the Trinity as the source of all power, as well as to "for thine is the power" in the Lord's Prayer. The Second Helvetic Confession offers an extensive discussion of church power as it relates to ministers,[10] which provides a theological rationale for the nature of the power that a minister has in the church of Jesus Christ.

> Now, therefore, it is fitting that we also say something about the power and duty of the ministers of the Church. Concerning this power some have argued industriously, and to it have subjected everything on earth, even the greatest things, and they have done so contrary to the commandment of the Lord who has prohibited dominion for his disciples and has highly commended humility (Luke 22:24ff.; Matt. 18:3ff.; 20:25ff.). There is, indeed, another power that is pure and absolute, which is called the power of right. According to this power all things in the whole world are subject to Christ, who is Lord of all, as he himself has testified when he said: "All authority in heaven and on earth has been given to me" (Matt. 28:18), and again, "I am the first and the last, and behold I am alive for evermore, and I have the keys of Hades and Death" (Rev. 1:18); also, "He has the key of David, which opens and no one shall shut, who shuts and no one opens" (Rev. 3:7).[11]

This passage begins the discussion by raising the question of the source of any minister's power. It suggests that power, according to Scripture, has been given to Jesus Christ, who has "highly commended humility" for his disciples, and "all authority" is reserved to the Lord of the church. Having laid this foundation, the focus shifts to the office of minister, in a paragraph that opens by identifying another power.

> *The Power of the Office and of the Minister.* Then there is another power of an office or of ministry limited by him who has full and absolute power. And this is more like a service than a dominion. *The Keys.* For a lord gives up his power to the steward in his house, and for that cause gives him the keys, that he may admit into or exclude from the house those whom his lord will have admitted or excluded. In virtue of this power the minister, because of his office, does that which the Lord has commanded him to do; and the Lord confirms what he does, and wills that what his servant has done will be so regarded and acknowledged, as if he himself had done it. Undoubtedly, it is to this that these evangelical sentences refer: "I will give you the keys of the kingdom of heaven, and whatever you bind on earth shall be bound in heaven, and whatever you loose on earth shall be loosed in heaven" (Matt. 16:19). Again, "If you forgive the sins of any, they are forgiven; if you retain

the sins of any, they are retained" (John 20:23). But if the minister does not carry out everything as the Lord has commanded him, but transgresses the bounds of faith, then the Lord certainly makes void what he has done. Wherefore the ecclesiastical power of the ministers of the Church is that function whereby they indeed govern the Church of God, but yet so do all things in the Church as the Lord has prescribed in his Word. When those things are done, the faithful esteem them as done by the Lord himself. But mention has already been made of the keys above.[12]

The "power of the keys" had been understood prior to the Reformation as a gift given to the church and its priests for determining entrance into heaven. This understanding has been reformed and herein emphasizes that a minister is a steward of the power of the keys. It is also stressed that stewardship of this power is appropriately exercised only when administered in accordance with scriptural principles. This is a reflection of what is understood today as limited authority.

Another limitation the Second Helvetic sets forth builds on the necessity of humility in stewards.

> *The Power of Ministers Is One and the Same, and Equal.* Now the one and an equal power or function is given to all ministers in the Church. Certainly, in the beginning, the bishops or presbyters governed the Church in common; no man lifted up himself above another, none usurped greater power or authority over his fellow-bishops. For remembering the words of the Lord: "Let the leader among you become as one who serves" (Luke 22:26), they kept themselves in humility, and by mutual services they helped one another in the governing and preserving of the Church.[13]

This understanding is what Presbyterians call "parity of ministry." It requires that all officers have an equal vote in the decisions of a governing body. There is also an emphasis upon mutuality of ministry, which is another characteristic of Presbyterian governance.

1b. "that is to say, that the Holy Scriptures are the only rule of faith and manners. . . ."

The second phrase of the seventh Historic Principle repeats a qualification regarding the exercise of church power that is consistent with what we have already seen. Although not directly from the *Book of Confessions*, there are three entries in the confessions with similar wording. The closest statement is found in the Westminster Confession, which closes the paragraph naming the canonical books of the Bible with, "All which [books] are given by inspiration of God, to be the rule of faith and life."[14] This suggests that, for those who profess to be Christians, church life, as all of life, is to fall under the guidance of Scripture. While the seventh Historic Principle specifically addresses church power, the conviction is also evident that God's sovereign rule extends over all of life, and that there is no area of life, particularly of church life, that is exempt from the commitment to seek to live as faithful stewards of all of God's gifts, which includes the gifts of power and authority.

As noted in chapter 3, the phrase "manner of life" is used in G-5.0106a. This is the phrase which, in its abstraction, has been a factor in the debate that led to the adoption of G-6.0106b. The 210th General Assembly adopted "Standards of Ethical Conduct"[15] for church members, ministers of the Word and Sacrament, elders and deacons, volunteers, and employees of the Presbyterian Church (U.S.A.). This code of ethics was developed in response to Overture 95–68 from the Presbytery of Western Reserve. The action taken by the General Assembly represented a revision of the original overture.[16] The specific action regarding this Code of Ethics was to:

> Approve the Standards of Ethical Conduct for Members of the Presbyterian Church (U.S.A.) and the Standards of Ethical Conduct for Employees and Volunteers of the Presbyterian Church (U.S.A.) for those serving in General Assembly entities and instruct those entities to include these standards in their personnel policies.

> Commend the Standards of Ethical Conduct together with References and Examples to presbyteries and synods as a model for their study, approval, and inclusion in their Manuals of Operation.[17]

This action demonstrates the seventh Historic Principle in action by its use of the word *commend*. This action, like most actions of the General Assembly, speaks to the rest of the church regarding what the governing body with commissioners from every presbytery have found to be their collective wisdom.

1c. ". . . that no Church governing body ought to pretend to make laws to bind the conscience in virtue of their own authority. . . ."

This clause is a reminder of the importance of the first Historic Principle and offers a caution about the temptations inherent within the power of governing bodies.

The general powers of governing bodies are identified in chapter IX of "Form of Government: Governing Bodies," section G-9.0102b. The general powers may be delineated as follows:

1. They may frame symbols of faith, bear testimony against error in doctrine and immorality in life;
2. resolve questions of doctrine and of discipline;
3. give counsel in matters of conscience;
4. and decide issues properly brought before them under the provisions of the *Book of Order*;

5. They may authorize the serving of the Lord's Supper in accordance with the principles of the Directory for Worship (W-2.4012, W-3.6204);
6. They have power to establish plans and rules for the worship, mission, government, and discipline of the church and to do those things necessary to the peace, purity, unity, and progress of the church under the will of Christ;
7. They have responsibility for the leadership, guidance, and government of that portion of the church which is under their jurisdiction.

These seven plenary powers belong to all governing bodies: session, presbytery, synod, and General Assembly. They cover the functions of witnessing to the gospel, deciding theological or faith questions, providing counsel regarding conscience, deciding issues in responsibilities assigned to them, administering communion, conducting worship for their body, planning for mission, and leading the church within their scope of responsibility.

The following paragraph sets forth how governing bodies are connected to one another.

All governing bodies of the church are united by the nature of the church and share with one another responsibilities, rights, and powers as provided in this Constitution. The governing bodies are separate and independent but have such mutual relations that the act of one of them is the act of the whole church performed by it through the appropriate governing body. The jurisdiction of each governing body is limited by the express provisions of the Constitution, with powers not mentioned being reserved to the presbyteries, and with the acts of each subject to review by the next higher governing body. (G-9.0103)

The key word here is "mutual."[18] This mutuality works because it is structured according to three important implications of the seventh Historic Principle. Express powers, the basic governing body, and review provide the framework for the so-called connectional system of Presbyterians and reflect the influence of the Constitution of the United States of America.

The phrase "express powers" of the U.S. Constitution (Section 8 of Article I) delineates the eighteen express powers of Congress. In similar fashion, the *Book of Order* defines specific responsibilities for each governing body, as shown in Table 4.

TABLE 4. RESPONSIBILITIES FOR EACH GOVERNING BODY

Governing body	Reference	Number of responsibilities
Session	G-10.0102	19
Presbytery	G-11.0103	27
Synod	G-12.0102	20
General Assembly	G-13.0103	24

While every governing body of the Presbyterian Church (U.S.A.) has more express powers than Congress, the responsibilities are much more specific. The specificity of responsibility lessens the likelihood that a governing body will attempt to make laws to bind the conscience.

The division of ninety specific responsibilities among the four governing bodies presents a challenge, especially when combined with the responsibility of each member of each governing body to ensure that no governing body act in an area specifically assigned to another governing body. For example, a presbytery may want to have a united service on some special occasion where every church in the presbytery worships together in one place. Were a presbytery to pass a motion to require every church to close its own service on that day so that all congregations could worship together, the presbytery would be taking the responsibility given to sessions in G-10.0102d and W-1.4004f.

It must also be recognized that these responsibilities are assigned to groups, not to individual persons. No one person may on his or her own initiative fulfill a responsibility given to a governing body in the *Book of Order*. There is a subtle difference between the respect or honor given to persons who have been installed into responsible positions, and the limited authority they may discharge. For example, the moderator of a governing body is respected by those who have chosen that candidate to preside at meetings. However, a moderator has no more authorized power than any other member, except to the degree that those are explicitly granted to every moderator. A pastor may, for example, be tempted to decide who will be baptized. While this may be justified for various reasons, it undermines the responsibility given the session to make such decisions (W-2.3011).

The wording of the phrase "with powers not mentioned being reserved to the presbyteries" may seem to run counter to what has just been proposed. This wording is strikingly similar to the Tenth Amendment to the Constitution of the United States, which reads: "The powers not delegated to the United States by the Constitution, nor prohibited by it to the States, are reserved to the States respectively, or to the people." These might be called "remainder clauses," as they serve a housekeeping task of cleaning up loose ends in both documents. The first articulation of this stipulation appears to have been in the Report of the Special Commission of 1925, usually called the Swearingen Commission, to the 1925 General Assembly, for the chairperson. At the beginning of its report regarding ordination, the report articulated seven principles, four of which provide background for understanding this "remainder clause:"

a. Supreme authority originating in the divine Head of the Church is communicated to the members directly by the Holy Spirit. On the human side, therefore this authority inheres in the people so enlightened and impelled by the Holy Spirit. This is the fundamental principle of Presbyterianism.

b. Beyond the particular church, the presbytery is the organizational unit and the seat of original authority.

c. The powers of the General Assembly are specific, delegated, and limited, having been conferred upon it by the presbyteries; whereas the powers of the presbyteries are general and inherent.

d. It follows that the powers of the General Assembly are enumerated and defined; but the powers of the presbytery, being reserved powers, are not necessarily fully enumerated nor strictly defined. Future conditions may call for the exercise of powers not now employed.[19]

This statement of principles remained a report until 1993 when the phrase was proposed by the Special Committee on the Nature of the Church and the Practice of Governance.[20] The wording was amended by the Advisory Committee on the Constitution,[21] passed by the General Assembly, and adopted by the presbyteries. As a rationale for the proposal, the Special Committee commented:

> It seems helpful for the presbytery, as the more inclusive governing body with the closest relations to the congregation, to have flexibility to respond quickly and efficiently to local issues. It seems unwise at this time to force uniformity.[22]

> In Reformed polity, no one governing body has been understood to be more important than another. Each carries specific responsibilities and the phrase "more inclusive" is used to indicate governing bodies with wider representation than others.[23]

Neither predecessor denomination had a statement regarding this issue in their respective constitutions.[24]

1d. ". . . and that all their decisions should be founded upon the revealed will of God."

Although the final clause of the first sentence of the seventh Historic Principle sounds again the hallmark of Protestants, faithfulness to this affirmation is often open to question. Its fulfillment requires more than affixing a Bible verse that seems to support a given decision. Governing bodies might well discuss and clarify how to take this clause seriously as they go about their business.

2a. "Now though it will easily be admitted that all synods and councils may err, through the frailty inseparable from humanity. . . ."

This first clause of the second sentence of the seventh Historic Principle echoes a statement found in the Westminster Confession regarding governing bodies.

> All synods or councils since the apostles' times, whether general or particular, may err, and many have erred; therefore they are not to be made the rule of faith or practice, but to be used as a help in both.[25]

The support for this statement in the text of the confession refers to a "General Note" that addresses the aforementioned concern that there be a scriptural base for governing body action.

> At several points the Confession of Faith is more specific in its statements than are the Scriptures. These statements are inferences drawn from the Scriptures or from statements based on the Scriptures, or from the experience and observation of the Church. In such cases no texts are cited, but reference is made to this General Note.[26]

This clause serves as a reminder that "synods and councils," which we today call governing bodies, are themselves open to error. The scope of representation in the governing body does not, in and of itself, protect the governing body from error.

> **2b. ". . . yet there is much greater danger from the usurped claim of making laws than from the right of judging upon laws already made, and common to all who profess the gospel . . ."**

Here is the heart of the second sentence and it is complex and challenging. It is bold in claiming that "the usurped claim of making laws" is more dangerous than reviewing laws already made by those who believe the gospel. Here again are noted the temptations of idolatry and tyranny (G-2.0500a(4)). This diagnosis of the problem of not adhering to the requirement of scriptural and confessional basis for decisions shines a bright light on the tendency to seek pragmatic, rather than exegetically and theologically sound solutions to problems.

> **2c. ". . . although this right, as necessity requires in the present state, be lodged with fallible men."**

The second sentence ends with a reminder that all humans are sinful, yet claims the broader base of the faithful as a corrective to human fallibility. This hope rests in the understanding of redemption in Christ, as well as in bearing in mind that:

> All things in Scripture are not alike plain in themselves, nor alike clear unto all; yet those things which are necessary to be known, believed, and observed, for salvation, are so clearly propounded and opened in some place of Scripture or other, that not only the learned, but the unlearned, in a due use of the ordinary means, may attain unto a sufficient understanding of them.[27]

There is a basic trust expressed in this chapter of the Westminster Confession regarding Scripture that "a due use of the ordinary means" by unlearned believers will produce a "sufficient understanding" so that whether or not something is consistent with Scripture is not a mystery, nor is discernment dependent upon someone with special expertise. There is revealed here a willingness to trust in the sensible consensus of believers.

The seventh Historic Principle may be summed up as teaching the importance of stewardship of Christ's gift of power for the ministry of the church. This gift can, has been, and will continue to be misused in various ways, however, the careful, mutual, respectful use of authorized power will result in fulfillment of its purpose, the glory of our Lord and Savior, Jesus Christ.

otes

1. See Max Weber, "The Types of Authority" in *The Theory of Social and Economic Organization*, translated by A. M. Henderson and Talcott Parsons (Glencoe, IL: Free Press, 1947), pp. 324–326 as cited in Talcott Parsons, et al., *Theories of Society*, vol. 1 (Glencoe, IL: Free Press, 1947), pp. 626–632.

2. Paul M. Harrison, *Authority and Power in a Free Church Tradition* (New Jersey: Princeton University Press, 1959), p. 4.

3. Ibid.

4. Ibid.

5. The principle has two sentences with 142 words, an average of 71 words per sentence. The readability rating puts it as appropriate for juniors in college.

6. The numbering scheme indicates the sentence by number, and the clause by letter. The text is G-1.0307.

7. William Little, *The Oxford English Dictionary on Historical Principles* (Oxford: Clarendon Press, 1955), p. 1255.

8. Ibid., p. 464.

9. Office of Worship, *The Worship of God*. Supplemental Liturgical Resource 5 (Philadelphia: The Westminster Press, 1987), p. 61.

10. Chapter XVIII "Of the Ministers of the Church, Their Institution, and Duties" (*Book of Confessions*, 5.142–168) is a comprehensive and surprisingly relevant treatment of this topic.

11. *Book of Confessions*, 5.157.

12. Ibid., 5.159.

13. Ibid., 5.160.

14. Ibid., 6.002. The other instances are 5.010, which speaks of testing interpretations of Scripture by the "rule of faith and love"; 6.175, which mentions the "rule of faith and practice"; and 7.113, which characterizes Scripture as "the only rule of faith and practice." The *Oxford English Dictionary on Historical Principles* indicates that "manners" can be understood as "the modes of life, rules of behavior, conditions of society, prevailing in a people" (p. 1201). The phrase "rule of faith and manners" is attributed to Archbishop John Tillotson, 1630–94.

15. *Minutes of the 210th General Assembly* (1998), 18.005–007.

16. The original overture is found in *Minutes of the 207th General Assembly* (1995), pp. 712–713. The action approved appears on pp. 80–81.

17. *Minutes of the 210th General Assembly* (1998), 43.023.

18. This repeats previous use of the term in G-1.0305 ("mutual forbearance") and in G-4.0302, ("mutual relationships") and is found again in G-9.0901 ("mutual work"). "Mutual" also appears in G-15.0302 regarding some ecumenical relationships ("mutual affirmation and admonition"), as well as twelve times in the "Directory for Worship" (1.1005b; 3.5302; 4.8002, 4.8003; 6.1000, 6.1002 [twice], 6.3001, 6.3002, 6.3011; 7.2002, 7.4003).

19. *Minutes of the 159th General Assembly* (1927), p. 62. Quoted in *The Presbyterian Constitution and Digest* (Philadelphia: Office of the General Assembly, 1963), vol. 2, p. A319. The argument is based on the historic development of the Presbyterians in America, where presbyteries were formed in 1706, synod in 1716, and General Assembly in 1789.

20. *Minutes of the 205th General Assembly* (1993), 26.221–222, p. 372. This entire report (pp. 355–400) offers a comprehensive view of Presbyterian polity.

21. Ibid., 21.051.

22. Ibid., par. 26.224.

23. Ibid., 26.225.

24. The *Book of Order: Annotated Edition* notes that the United Presbyterian Church of North America had a provision that unspecified powers belonged to the General Assembly.

25. *Book of Confessions*, 6.175.

26. Ibid., p. 169.

27. Ibid., 6.007.

9

Decency, Order, and Discipline (G-1.0308)

> The life of a Christian is empowered by grace, is expressed in obedience, and is shaped by discipline.
>
> —*Book of Order*, W-5.1004

The eighth Historic Principle completes a circle, returning to issues of decency and order, adding an additional aspect to the exploration as it provides a sobering, even challenging conclusion to the principles of church order.

> Lastly, that if the preceding scriptural and rational principles be steadfastly adhered to, the vigor and strictness of its discipline will contribute to the glory and happiness of any church. Since ecclesiastical discipline must be purely moral or spiritual in its object, and not attended with any civil effects, it can derive no force whatever but from its own justice, the approbation of an impartial public, and the countenance and blessing of the great Head of the Church universal. (G-1.0308)

The conditional clause in the first sentence of the eighth Historic Principle, "if the preceding scriptural and rational principles be steadfastly adhered to," provides a challenge. The drafters of these principles left their work to those who would bear responsibility for the new entity that they were designing. They were willing to entrust their work to those who followed, in the hope that their principles would continue to bear good fruit in generations to come. The phrase "steadfastly adhered to" would make more sense for contemporary readers if the word *conscientious* were substituted for it. This would also connect it with the first Historic Principle.

The eighth Historic Principle asserts that the principles are both scriptural and rational, echoing the thoughtful process of developing principles of order for church life that are articulated in G-1.0100c: "Matters are to be ordered according to the Word by reason and sound judgment, under the guidance of the Holy Spirit." It is a confession that their work was guided by God's Holy Spirit in a way that did not bypass their rational capabilities, but used such processes to arrive at principles designed to function to God's glory for some time to come. Some humility is also evident in the admission that the work is their best, and is likely to work as intended only if those who follow in their train accept and use these principles in their life together.

The subject of the first sentence plunges the reader into what may not be readily comprehended when it states: "The vigor and strictness of its discipline will contribute to the glory and happiness of any church." The word *discipline* is generally understood in terms of punishment. In academic life, a discipline is a distinctive sphere of study. When we identify ourselves as disciples of Jesus Christ in our baptism, we accept the discipline of living according to the instruction of our Lord. The epigraph for this chapter succinctly expresses this understanding of discipline as a critically important aspect of the Christian life.[1]

The overtone of education in the term *discipline* is true to the Greek word παιδεια (*paideia*), which is used in the New Testament in reference to instruction and discipline.[2] Hebrews 12:5–10 refers to Prov. 3:11–12 in a discussion of discipline, where the reference is to God who exercises discipline in order to educate God's people. In Rom. 2:20, Paul speaks of God's law as a "teacher of children." Second Timothy 3:16 indicates that one role of Scripture is "for training in righteousness."

Paul's careful discussion of the function of God's law in Gal. 3:10–29 is important for understanding the word *discipline*. Paul asks, "Is the law then opposed to the promises of God?" Paul's response to his own question is, "Certainly not"(Gal. 3:21). Paul's discussion led John Calvin to propose a "third use of the law." While the law is "the best instrument for them to learn more thoroughly the nature of the Lord's will to which they aspire," Calvin also proposed that "we need not only teaching but exhortation."[3] Calvin understood Scripture as teaching that God's way of dealing with God's people is complex and multifaceted.[4] So God's law disciplines us in the sense of warning us of things that are contrary to God's will, helping us understand that God corrects and admonishes us when we fall short of God's purpose, and offering us positive guidance in those things which please God.

Another note struck by Calvin is apparent in the Scots Confession treatment of how a believer can differentiate a true church from a false one.

> The notes of the true Kirk, therefore, we believe, confess, and avow to be: first, the true preaching of the Word of God, in which God has revealed himself to us, as the writings of the prophets and apostles declare; secondly, the right administration of the sacraments of Christ Jesus, with which must be associated the Word and promise of God to seal and confirm them in our hearts; and lastly, ecclesiastical discipline uprightly ministered, as God's Word prescribes, whereby vice is repressed and virtue nourished.[5]

The role of discipline was added by Calvin, apparently in light of what had happened in the life of the church prior to the Reformation. The eighth Historic Principle is a restatement of this Reformed theological tenet.

It was noted in chapter 8 that there was a distinctive understanding of "the power of the keys" in the *Book of Confessions*. The Heidelberg Catechism has two questions whose responses bear directly on the role of discipline in the church.

Q. 83. What is the office of the keys?
A. The preaching of the holy gospel and Christian discipline. By these two means the kingdom of heaven is opened to believers and shut against unbelievers.[6]

Q. 85. How is the kingdom of heaven shut and opened by Christian discipline?
A. In this way: Christ commanded that those who bear the Christian name in an unchristian way either in doctrine or in life should be given brotherly admonition. If they do not give up their errors or evil ways, notification is given to the church or to those ordained for this by the church. Then, if they do not change after this warning, they are forbidden to partake of the holy Sacraments and are thus excluded from the communion of the church and by God himself from the kingdom of Christ. However, if they promise and show real amendment, they are received again as members of Christ and of the church.[7]

Discipline here is discussed as "brotherly admonition," a phrase that somewhat softens the sense of discipline, as it is often understood.

The Second Helvetic Confession devotes a paragraph to discipline that reviews ecclesiastical application and relies on Bible references as the basis for its teaching.

Discipline. And since discipline is an absolute necessity in the Church and excommunication was once used in the time of the early fathers, and there were ecclesiastical judgments among the people of God, wherein this discipline was exercised by wise and godly men, it also falls to ministers to regulate this discipline for edification, according to the circumstances of the time, public state, and necessity. At all times and in all places the rule is to be observed that everything is to be done for edification, decently and honorably, without oppression and strife. For the apostle testifies that authority in the Church was given to him by the Lord for building up and not for destroying (2 Cor. 10:8). And the Lord himself forbade the weeds to be plucked up in the Lord's field, because there would be danger lest the wheat also be plucked up with it (Matt. 13:29ff.).[8]

This extensive discussion of the role of discipline provides the confessional foundation for the understanding of discipline present in the eighth Historic Principle and in the rest of the *Book of Order*. The phrase "the vigor and strictness of its discipline will contribute to the glory and happiness of any church," from the first sentence of the eighth Historic Principle, may initially startle the reader with its harsh-sounding and seemingly unyielding terms. However, the passages from Scripture and the *Book of Confessions* suggest that what the drafters had in mind could be expressed in contemporary language as "with diligence and fairness." These terms are more comprehensible to modern ears and are in concert with the remainder of the principle.

The second sentence of the eighth Historic Principle sets further parameters for the practice of church discipline. Reference is to *ecclesiastical* discipline, making explicit that what is under consideration is discipline within the church. Furthermore, the purpose of ecclesiastical discipline is described as "purely moral or spiritual in its object." This phrase is developed more fully in two other places.

The first is within chapter IV of "Form of Government"; "The Church and Its Unity," in the listing of Principles of Presbyterian Government.

> Ecclesiastical jurisdiction is a shared power, to be exercised jointly by presbyters gathered in governing bodies. (G-4.0301h)

One implication of the informal exercise of ecclesiastical discipline is demonstrated by one of the responsibilities given to the session:

> To maintain regular and continuing relationship to the higher governing bodies of the church, including . . . (6) proposing to the presbytery and, through it, to the synod and the General Assembly such measures as may be of common concern to the mission of the whole church. (G-10.0102p)

This quasi-formal provision is the basis for the many overtures to the General Assembly that emerge year after year. However, the caveat in this provision that it be a topic of "common concern to the *mission* of the *whole* church" (italics added), is sometimes overlooked.

A second, more extensive elaboration on the terms "moral" and "spiritual" is found in the preamble to the "Rules of Discipline."

> The power that Jesus Christ has vested in his Church, a power manifested in the exercise of church discipline, is one for building up the body of Christ, not for destroying it, for redeeming, not for punishing. It should be exercised as a dispensation of mercy and not of wrath so that the great ends of the Church may be achieved, that all children of God may be presented faultless in the day of Christ. (D-1.0102)

This clear, evangelical, and redemptive statement restates the scriptural and confessional basis for church discipline. The preceding paragraph makes a similar point while providing a detailed description of the way Presbyterians approach ecclesiastical discipline.

> Church discipline is the church's exercise of authority given by Christ, both in the direction of guidance, control, and nurture of its members and in the direction of constructive criticism of offenders. Thus, the purpose of discipline is to honor God by making clear the significance of membership in the body of Christ; to preserve the purity of the church by nourishing the individual within the life of the believing community; to correct or restrain wrongdoing in order to bring members to repentance and restoration; to restore the unity of the church by removing the causes of discord and division; and to secure the just, speedy, and economical determination of proceedings. In all respects, members are to be accorded procedural safeguards and due process, and it is the intention of these rules so to provide.[9] (D-1.0101)

The words "the church's exercise of authority given by Christ," provide yet another reminder that authority in the church is a gift from our Lord for doing the work appropriate to the church. The preamble then suggests two directions for the church's exercise of the authority given by Christ in the practice of ecclesiastical discipline. The first direction is defined as "guidance, control, and nurture," which are three words not often put together. There may be a tendency to focus on "control" and thus to fear that this introduces something contrary to the first Historic Principle's insistence on freedom of conscience. However, the context provided by the words *guidance* and *nurture* makes it clear that this is a gentle, pastoral, sort of control.

The other direction, "constructive criticism of offenders," reminds one of Paul's call to believers to speak "the truth in love" (Eph. 4:15). The implication here is that discipline has an educative, rather than punitive function with the goal of helping the community grow in their obedience to our Lord.

Discipline in terms of the eighth Historic Principle must be divided into informal and formal disciplinary mechanisms. Most of the discipline addressed by this principle takes place informally in the course of life as a community of faith. People speak with one another in ways that support positive behavior and question those behaviors that seem inappropriate. Since all members are engaged in ministry, interaction within the community resolves a great deal of what otherwise would become issues of discipline. This dynamic within the community of faith is the practical evidence of the priesthood of all believers, a hallmark of the Reformation.

The other, formal approach to discipline might be considered as "industrial-strength pastoral care." The Principles of Presbyterian Government alludes to this formal system.

> A higher governing body shall have the right of review and control over a lower one and shall have power to determine matters of controversy upon reference, complaint, or appeal. (G-4.0301f)

The word *reference* is defined as:

> A written request, made by a session or a permanent judicial commission of a presbytery or synod to the permanent judicial commission of the next higher governing body, for trial and decision or a hearing on appeal in a remedial or disciplinary case not yet decided. (D-4.0101)[10]

The "Rules of Discipline" present the way the formal disciplinary process proceeds. Most Presbyterians never encounter formal discipline. The only decisions made broadly public are those cases that are appealed to the Permanent Judicial Commission of the General Assembly. These decisions are printed in the *Minutes of the General Assembly*.

The formal disciplinary system has two types of cases: remedial and disciplinary (D-2.0201). "A *remedial case* is one in which an irregularity ["an erroneous decision or action"] or a delinquency ["an omission or failure to act"] of a lower governing body, the General Assembly Council, or an entity of the General Assembly may be corrected by a higher governing body."[11] *Remedial* here is used in the sense of finding a remedy to an act of a governing body that was wrongly decided, or that was not considered as it should have been. Filing such a case requires that a remedy be specified in the complaint. The governing body must also be asked to correct the alleged error or delinquency before filing the complaint.

"A *disciplinary case* is one in which a church member or officer may be censured for an offense" (D-2.0203), which is defined as, "any act or omission by a member or officer of the church that is contrary to the Scriptures or the *Constitution of the Presbyterian Church (U.S.A.)*."[12] Charges must be filed in order to initiate a disciplinary case.[13] A disciplinary case is more serious and deals with any Presbyterian who directly violates that which is required by the church. If a person is found guilty by a trial, "The degrees of church censure are rebuke, rebuke with supervised rehabilitation, temporary exclusion from exercise of ordained office or membership, and removal from ordained office or membership."[14] Such cases are infrequent.

Lest the two general directions do not provide sufficient operational clarity, D-1.0101 outlines five more specific requirements so that the disciplinary process will accomplish its purpose to honor God. These five requirements are as follows:

1. "making clear the significance of membership in the body of Christ . . ." What does it mean to belong to the church today? There is the boundary called membership to be maintained with care, not to protect the institution, but to make clear to all that the church is a unique institution, different from other voluntary organizations because of its members' commitment to Jesus Christ.

2. "to preserve the purity of the church by nourishing the individual within the life of the believing community . . ." The focus is on the health of the believing community, rather than on the individual. Purity provides a reminder that the church is the instrumentality of Jesus Christ.

3. "to correct or restrain wrongdoing in order to bring members to repentance and restoration . . ." The pastoral task of correcting wrongdoing again focuses on maintaining a healthy fellowship through the most effective, yet gentle means.

4. "to restore the unity of the church by removing the causes of discord and division . . ." Discord and division within a fellowship are assumed to be spiritual problems, rather than sociological or psychological ills. Otherwise, the healing power of Christ would not seem an appropriate way of resolving the difficulty.

5. "to secure the just, speedy, and economical determination of proceedings. . . ." This final purpose needs to be taken as a relative statement, since the three suggested qualities are not easily reconciled. It is also important to bear in mind that a deliberate process is preferable to having no means for resolving difficulties.

The final sentence of the first paragraph of the preamble to the Principles of Church Discipline offers a final condition that is intended to serve as reassurance regarding the nature of the disciplinary process: "In all respects, members are to be accorded procedural safeguards and due process, and it is the intention of these rules so to provide." While the "Rules of Discipline" are admittedly detailed and technical, their detail is intended to ensure that anyone involved in the disciplinary process can expect procedural equality through provisions that are public.

The second sentence of the eighth Historic Principle states that ecclesiastical discipline must not be attended with any civil effects. Presbyterian heritage lies behind this prohibition. In addition to similar language in the first Historic Principle, this point is also stressed in the discussion of governing bodies.

> Since ecclesiastical discipline must be purely moral or spiritual in its object, and not attended with any civil effects, it can derive no force whatever but from its own justice, the approbation of an impartial public, and the countenance and blessing of the great Head of the Church universal. (G-1.0308)

This careful segregation of church from state is consistent with the First Amendment to the Constitution of the United States. It is also evidence of the suffering of many Presbyterians prior to crossing the Atlantic who were harassed, tried, and often imprisoned for their faith. This historical experience has continued to affect Presbyterians, sustaining a belief that the church has a message for civil governments as well as for the faithful.[15]

The eighth Historic Principle provides a rousing crescendo at the end of the Historic Principles (G-1.0308). Ecclesiastical discipline has force and effect only to the degree that it results in the three following qualities:

1. ". . . its own justice . . ." This should be self-evident: a church that had a formal disciplinary system that was inherently unjust would be a detriment to the community. Whatever system is adopted, the community must determine that decisions from that system are just, even when they are not popular.

2. ". . . the approbation of an impartial public . . ." Justice must be perceived by the faithful but even more so by bystanders whose awareness of the church is minimal, and who have no vested interest in the outcome. This component keeps the system from becoming entrenched.

3. ". . . the countenance and blessing of the great Head of the Church universal." The final quality reminds Presbyterians that in discipline, as in every other activity in which the church engages, the bottom line is whether Jesus Christ is honored.

It seems fitting to close this discussion of church discipline with Jesus' teaching on judgment as recorded in Matt. 7:1–2.

Do not judge, so that you may not be judged. For with the judgment you make you will be judged, and the measure you give will be the measure you get.

otes

1. Note also that W-5.5000 addresses "other disciplines in personal worship and discipleship."

2. Used eight times in its noun form, thirteen times in verb form, παιδευω (*paideuo*). Eight of these occurrences are in Heb. 11:5–10. Rev. W. F. Moulton and Rev. A. S. Geden, ed., *A Concordance to the Greek New Testament* (Edinburgh: T. & T. Clark, 1963), pp. 745–756.

3. John Calvin, *Institutes of the Christian Religion*, edited by John T. McNeill and translated by Ford Lewis Battles (Philadelphia: The Westminster Press, 1960), II.VII.12, p. 360.

4. A thoughtful discussion of παιδεια (*paideia*) can be found in Georg Bertram, "The Paideia Concept in the New Testament," in *Theological Dictionary of the New Testament*, edited by Gerhard Friedrich, vol. 5 (Grand Rapids: Wm. B. Eerdmans Publishing Co., 1967), pp. 619–625.

5. *Book of Confessions*, 3.18.

6. *Book of Confessions*, 4.083.

7. Ibid., 4.085. The intervening question relates to how preaching functions in this context.

8. Ibid., 5.165. Other passages referring to discipline not noted here are as follows: 4.104; 5.096, 5.167, 5.216, 5.227, 5.254; 6.129; 7.218.

9. These two paragraphs must be read aloud at the beginning of every trial. See D-7.0401a and D-11.0402a.

10. The terms, complaint and appeal, will be discussed later.

11. D-2.0202. Bracketed material is from D-2.0203a and b.

12. See D-2.0203 and D-2.0203b.

13. D-10.0400 provides the detail process involved.

14. D-12.0101. These degrees are further defined in D-12.0000, together with provisions for restoration from these censures.

15. James H. Smylie, *A Brief History of the Presbyterians* (Louisville: Geneva Press, 1996), pp. 36–38, hints at this history.

Connecting Presbyterians (G-1.0400)

$\mathcal{P}$resbyterians often speak of their of government as a "connectional system," carried out by governing bodies.[1]

> The Presbyterian Church (U.S.A.) shall be governed by representative bodies composed of presbyters, both elders and Ministers of the Word and Sacrament. These *governing bodies* shall be called
>
> > session
> > presbytery
> > synod
> > General Assembly.[2]

The provision clearly identifies what the governing bodies are, but the more challenging issue is how these various bodies are connected to one another. That question brings up one important remaining foundational aspect of the polity of the Presbyterian Church (U.S.A.).

The Historic Principles of Church Government (G-1.0400) date from 1797, when they were adopted by the General Assembly. They appear as one paragraph, which may be why they are often overlooked. They are, in fact, the axioms on which Presbyterian polity rest. In fact, these are called *radical* principles of church government and discipline.[3] Without these axioms, the rest would appear to be a maze of rules. These axioms provide clarity on how Presbyterians are distinctive in their polity. For purposes of discussion, they will be approached one at a time.

1. **The several different congregations of believers, taken collectively, constitute one Church of Christ, called emphatically the Church . . .**

A pastor colleague once asked me, "What is it that ties the Presbyterian Church together?" We had been discussing the differences that kept arising and troubling our church. He wondered if it were merely the *Book of Order* that held the church together. We reviewed several other possibilities, which included the telephone, which is used for all sorts of communication among the various entities of the church.[4] Our conclusion was that the answer probably included numerous complex factors, the most important of which could not be teased out—except, of course, the Holy Spirit.

The first axiom of church government asserts church unity as a matter of belief. The statement suggests that congregations of believers usually have a strong sense of community. An appreciation of the local congregation is expressed in another way in "Form of Government," chapter VII, "The Particular Church."

> The particular church carries a vital responsibility in the mission of the church. There God's people perform especially the ministries of worship, proclamation, sharing the Sacraments, evangelism, nurture, counseling, personal and social healing, and service. Without this basic ministry to persons, neighborhoods, and communities, and the support given at the congregational level through prayer, personnel, and money, any other significant ministry of the church becomes impossible. Congregations serve as essential mission arms of the presbytery and of the larger church. (G-7.0102)

The phrase "vital responsibility in the mission" points to the essential nature of the role of the congregation, while the statement delineates the mission tasks the congregation is uniquely qualified to fulfill. A stronger statement regarding the congregation would be hard to find.

These congregations of believers are understood together as "one Church of Christ." There is a concern for balance demonstrated here, which reflects an appreciation of the tendency to value either the congregation on the one hand or the denomination on the other. Maintaining this balance, as difficult and perilous as that may be, is a continuing issue that the church faces as it goes about its mission.

The concern for balance was not merely a function of diversity in America. Prior to the emergence of denominations in the United States, the issue of how the church witnesses to its oneness in Christ had been an issue. It had its roots in the Reformation, when the issue of what constituted a church was pressing. For example, the Second Helvetic Confession, while affirming that there is only one church, states that

> The Church is divided into different parts or forms; not because it is divided or rent asunder in itself, but rather because it is distinguished by the diversity of the numbers that are in it.[5]

> Moreover, the Church Militant upon the earth has always had many particular churches. Yet all these are to be referred to the unity of the catholic Church.[6]

The Presbyterian struggle to balance the denomination and the local church is not the only possible response to this issue. It is, however, the Presbyterian conviction that those congregations that share the Presbyterian name are, in a real sense, "one Church of Christ." This conviction includes an understanding of "the communion of the saints,"[7] which celebrates the fellowship of those who are members of the body of Christ in all areas of the world at all times and places. This sense of being together may be why so many Presbyterians over the years have sung with particular gusto the phrase from "Onward Christian Soldiers": "We are not divided, all one body we, One in hope and doctrine, One in charity."[8]

2. **that a larger part of the Church, or a representation of it, should govern a smaller, or determine matters of controversy which arise therein;**

This axiom expresses an organizational principle that also applies to our Federal constitution. Representative government rests on an orderly broadening base of decision making. There is a significant difference between pure democracy, where everyone votes on every decision, and representative democracy, where the people elect persons to make decisions in specified areas of life. The Presbyterian Church is a representative democracy in this sense.

There is, however, an important distinction in how Presbyterians understand the function of those they elect to positions of responsibility. As noted earlier, the "Principles of Presbyterian Government" include the provision that "presbyters are not simply to reflect the will of the people, but rather to seek together to find and represent the will of Christ" (G-4.0301d). Persons elected to serve in governing bodies beyond the session are called "commissioners," which indicates that they are sent, not for the purpose of doing the bidding of those who send them, but rather to seek God's purpose within a body that represents a wider area of the church. The term *larger* here is used by Presbyterians to indicate a more inclusive governing body, referring to the broader base from which commissioners are elected. This approach replaces an earlier tendency to refer to higher governing bodies, which was interpreted hierarchically. It takes much more time to make decisions at these more inclusive levels than in congregations. Because these more inclusive bodies relate to larger geographical areas, they meet less frequently and are less directly engaged in the daily life of particular churches.

The scope of decisions that a more inclusive governing body is authorized to determine is specified in the *Book of Order*. The only governing body that may go beyond these limitations is the presbytery, and then only when that responsibility has not been assigned to another governing body. This ascending responsibility is what usually comes to mind when the phrase "connectional system" is used by Presbyterians.[9] Those who come from churches with congregational polity, where the congregation determines the degree to which a particular church will abide by decisions of other levels, may find it difficult to accept this axiom of Presbyterian government.

3. **that, in like manner, a representation of the whole should govern and determine in regard to every part, and to all the parts united:**

This axiom reiterates, and extends the previous axiom and adds a sense of corporate wholeness, suggesting dynamic interaction. The late–eighteenth-century phrase "in regard to every part, and to all the parts united" may startle contemporary readers with its very modern sound, which resonates with current concern about systems and interaction. This axiom also illustrates how seriously the balance between denomination and congregations is taken, as does a 1993 opinion of the Permanent Judicial Commission that included the radical principles in their decision.

> Under the radical principles, a presbytery (or any governing body) is not free to exercise its own judgment contrary to our constitutional standards or the lawful injunctions of higher governing bodies without jeopardizing the entire fabric of our Presbyterian system.
>
> The responsibilities of a presbytery in the calling process go beyond ensuring that prescribed steps are taken in the proper order. When finding the call of a congregation in order, it is the responsibility of a presbytery, through its committee on ministry, to offer counsel regarding the standards that represent the "voice of the whole Church."[10]

This relatedness is not an organizational principle derived from experience, rather it is drawn from scriptural insight and from a theological understanding of the living community of faith. It is conceivable that the drafters were expressing, in an abbreviated form, their understanding of the apostle Paul's metaphor of the church as the body of Christ.[11] They were sufficiently bold to apply the metaphor to their newly formed denomination in an effort to evoke commitment to the Presbyterian Church as a body of Christ, at the very least from a functional perspective. Inherent in these passages is the sense that there is a dynamic functional interconnection within the church.

The connectional system should trigger an awareness that we are members of the body of Christ, or as Paul put it in Rom. 12:5, "individually we are members one of another." Rather than being an abstract doctrine, this affirmation is for modern Presbyterians as much as it was for the new churches to whom Paul wrote, the practical foundation for how sister and brother believers are to approach one another in their interactions.

4.   **that is, that a majority shall govern;**

This axiom of democratic process has generated considerable discussion in recent years. There are proposals for "super majorities" regarding certain issues in politics. There appears to be a growing sense that a simple majority (more than one half) is inadequate for approving motions regarding difficult issues.

This axiom is expanded somewhat in the Principles of Presbyterian Government.

> Decisions shall be reached in governing bodies by vote, following opportunity for discussion, and a majority shall govern. . . . (G-4.0301e)

The phrase "following opportunity for discussion" adds a theological dimension to this axiom. *Discussion* is understood by Presbyterians as the opportunity for dynamic interchange of perspectives. Discussion provides the opportunity for clarification of issues, as well as providing time for the Holy Spirit to work in the hearts and minds of those present. This dynamic theological dimension all too often seems to get lost in the focus on business, in the politicization and polarization of discussion of viewpoints, or even in unquestioning acceptance of reports.

There are some situations in which a majority is considered insufficient. When there is a proposed amendment to the *Book of Confessions*, for example, two-thirds of the presbyteries must concur (G-18.0201a(2)). If a "significant minority of the voters are averse to the [pastoral] nominee," the congregation may choose not to prosecute the call. If, however, the majority insist on their right to call the pastor, there is a procedure for notifying the presbytery and the nominee of the "number of those who do not concur in the call and any other facts of importance" (G-14.0505). *Robert's Rules of Order* indicates that:

> The rules of parliamentary law found in this book will, on analysis, be seen to be constructed upon a careful balance of the rights of persons or of subgroups within an organization's or an assembly's total membership. That is, these rules are based on a regard for the rights:
>
> - of the majority,
> - of the minority, especially a strong minority—greater than one third,
> - of individual members,
> - of absentees, and
> - of all of these together.[12]

From a theological perspective, the protection of interests is understood as a necessary practice for members of the body of Christ who are obliged not to damage, through thoughtlessness, any of our brother and sister Christians.[13]

5.   . . . consequently that appeals may be carried from lower to higher governing bodies, till they be finally decided by the collected wisdom and united voice of the whole Church.

This fifth axiom acknowledges the potential of problems and provides for their resolution. This axiom combines the importance of discussion with the commitment to seek broader-based decisions. Appeals, as referred to in this axiom, has both a formal and an informal sense. In both senses, there is evidence of an assurance that there are resources beyond individual abilities when difficulties arise. Individuals need not bear the weight of difficulties alone.

The three-part contract between a pastor, a congregation, and a presbytery provides one example of how Presbyterians can work together to resolve tensions before they become problems.[14] There are also numerous staff persons throughout the denomination who serve as resources. These informal personal connections reflect some of the benefits of our Presbyterian system. "Ask and you shall receive" is good practice for Presbyterians in church life. Such informal means function most effectively when difficulties begin to emerge.[15]

The understanding of the church as the body of Christ, as discussed above, informs the way Presbyterians go about resolving differences. As a community that believes in one who died on a cross as the way to reconcile human beings with God, we must be about a ministry of reconciliation with one another. That does not mean giving in, but rather means obeying Jesus' new commandment:

> . . . that you love one another as I have loved you. No one has greater love than this, to lay down one's life for one's friends. (John 15:12–13)

Such self-giving love should be the motivation of relationships between all Christians, between all Presbyterians, and between the various entities of the Presbyterian Church (U.S.A.). For those charged to spread the good news, the willingness to struggle through the difficult issues of life in the church is essential for a faithful witness and mission.

6. **For these principles and this procedure, the example of the apostles and the practice of the primitive Church are considered as authority.**

The final axiom defines the authority of the Presbyterian Church (U.S.A.) and in so doing echoes something encountered earlier in G-1.0100c.

> In the worship and service of God and the government of the church, matters are to be ordered according to the Word by reason and sound judgment, under the guidance of the Holy Spirit.

The axiom ends where a strictly logical presentation might have begun. However, we may also understand this as a hymn of praise and thanksgiving to Almighty God for the gifts of Scripture and the devoted and disciplined reflection of those who gave us these axioms. The vital question for Presbyterians is whether, and to what degree, we will prove to be good stewards of this heritage.

otes

1. *Connectional system* is not, however, a term unique to Presbyterians. What is distinctive for Presbyterians is the representative aspect of equality of ministers of Word and Sacrament and elders in governing bodies beyond the session. A better term is *relational system.*

2. G-9.0101; italics added. In the United Presbyterian Church ("northern stream") these were called "judicatories." In the Presbyterian Church in the United States ("southern stream"), these were referred to as "church courts."

3. A footnote to G-1.0400 explains that "the word *radical* is used in its primary meaning of 'fundamental and basic.' "

4. Were the conversation to happen now, we would have to mention PresbyNet, the on-line service that provides for conversation as well as communication.

5. *Book of Confessions,* 5.127.

6. Ibid., 5.128.

7. "Communion of saints" appears as a phrase in *Book of Confessions,* 2.3 and 4.023. The doctrine is explained in 4.055, 5.125, 6.146–148, and 7.173.

8. Sabine Baring-Gould, "Onward Christian Soldiers," in *The Hymnbook,* no. 350 (Richmond: Presbyterian Church in the United States, 1955), p. 350.

9. The traditional phrase was ". . . a series of courts in a regular gradation."

10. *Sallade et al. vs. Presbytery of Genesee Valley,* in *Minutes of the 205th General Assembly* (1993), p. 168.

11. See Rom. 12:4–8; 1 Cor. 12:12–27; and Eph. 4:4–16 for three major instances.

12. Henry M. Robert, *Robert's Rules of Order: Newly Revised* (New York: ScottForesman, 1990), p. xliv. See G-9.0302, which names this resource as the authoritative guide for meetings.

13. The problem of how members are to treat one another is not new. See Matt. 20:20–28, 1 Cor. 1:10–17, and Gal. 5:13–15. Parallels indicate that controversy among the disciples was also a reality.

14. See G-11.0503j in this regard.

15. See chapter 9 of this book for an introduction to the Presbyterian system of discipline.

11
An Epilogue

This project has offered a constitutional view on Presbyterian polity. It could also be called a multidimensional approach, since I have taken the position that Presbyterian polity cannot be fully understood on the basis of the *Book of Order* by itself. This work has demonstrated how the Historic Principles of Church Order, along with biblical and confessional connections, provide a way of making sense of the *Book of Order*.

We have seen that the Historic Principles of Church Order point to persistent tensions of church life and identify issues of faith and order that emerge in various forms at different times in history. The Principles, therefore, serve as caution signs, preparing us for these tensions and issues that may house perils to the integrity of faith. The *Book of Order* has become, in this presentation, a historical commentary on what it means to be a community of faith as the body of Christ. Far from being merely a compendium of church law, the *Book of Order* is a guide for disciples seeking to be faithful within a particular community of faith.

With this perspective in mind, let us revisit the major themes of each chapter and consider the tensions suggested by the Historic Principles of Church Order. That the Historic Principles of Church Order identify tensions that continue to emerge in church life two centuries later is evidence of the considerable wisdom in these gems of our Presbyterian heritage. Although these tensions are sometimes cited as evidence of the illogic inherent in the *Book of Order*, I contend that they provide a valuable service. These tensions in church life alert us to the humanness of the church, to the impossibility of designing a "City of God" on this planet, to our imperfections even when we are at our best, to our need for redemption, and to our debt of gratitude to God for sending Jesus Christ as the one who brings new life. These tensions also provide a warning that there are some areas of life together in the church where we must proceed very carefully, lest we risk damaging other disciples, who are precious in God's eyes. There is also vitality in the tensions found in the *Book of Order*. Life in the Presbyterian way is a continuing challenge in which we seek to adapt a worthy heritage to meet the challenges of today and tomorrow. The tensions provide us with signposts for navigating life together as Presbyterians as we seek to lead a life worthy of the calling to which we have been called.[1]

The tension between *conscience* and *community* was identified in chapter 2. Our understanding of conscience is that it is a matter of interplay between an individual and community. Both are necessary, yet tensions arise. There is also a tension between the negative conscience, which warns us not to do some things, and positive or transformed conscience, which provides the internal drive for mission. We are admonished when dealing with this volatile area to remember that God alone is the Lord of conscience.

Community alerts us to the tension between being citizens of the United States of America and at the same time living in the realm of heaven. What does it mean for Presbyterians today to be in but not of the world? Deciding how to manage this "dual citizenship" is challenging in many ways, which often reflects individual experiences and age. A related tension is that of how one relates with integrity to any group. Commitment to Jesus Christ involves commitment to a community that is devoted to Jesus Christ as Lord and Savior. The issues of conscience and community raise awareness of the struggle we all face in determining our participation in a particular faith community. This commitment is so serious that Presbyterian polity provides for a person to leave our fellowship with the simple declaration that he or she no longer wishes to be a part of the community.

This survey of conscience/community issues demonstrates why our predecessors put this principle first in their list. Respect for conscience is an essential foundation for a lively body of the faithful moving forward together. The transformed conscience becomes the basis for humble faith in community, where the hallmark is to extend the good news into all areas of human life.

Chapter 4 discussed the tensions that revolve around the need for the community to make decisions and to live with the consequences of those decisions. The first decision a believer makes is whether to become part of a particular fellowship. That desire begins in the heart of the believer. The community has a responsibility to provide sufficient information about their fellowship in order that the decision be appropriately informed.

The Presbyterian community elects officers to whom it gives the authority to make decisions within certain explicit limits. Tension arises when the fellowship agrees that all members are eligible to vote and to be elected to office, yet there are qualifications that may exclude some members from office. One potential consequence is the hurt feelings of those not chosen to serve as officers.

Presbyterian organization rests on the basis of assigned and limited responsibilities. Within the defined limits, the officers are responsible to decide issues that arise. Another consequence is that, within their sphere, officers have a right to be wrong. While there are ways to protect members from violations of limits and process, the "buck stops" with the group discharging the responsibility.

Presbyterians openly affirm the right of Christians to determine the way they will live together, engage in mission, and make their decisions. Once there is a denomination, and a fellowship connects with that denomination, there are disciplines, and a new dimension of mutuality that serves to connect the fellowships into one church. Such connection serves to define the scope of decisions in order to maintain cohesiveness for the body.

The ultimate determiner of what is right and wrong is, of course, God. Presbyterians seek to make decisions under the guidance of God's Spirit and their understanding of Scripture and the *Book of Confessions*. These decisions reflect the best efforts of those selected as officers. There is always room for debate, more room, in fact, than is often used. There is also a balance of power in Presbyterian polity, similar to that of the government of the United States of America. Policy decisions are made by groups, not by individuals. These groups are accountable to the whole church. Once the body has acted, the question is settled, and those who disagree with the decision either accept the action (actively or passively) or face the question of whether or not they must seek another fellowship.

In the contemporary world, Presbyterian polity recognizes that there are consequences for all human decisions. Many decisions have unforeseen consequences. Some are more costly than could be anticipated. Decisions may come to be seen as erroneous, but until there has been an orderly review by an authorized group, the decision stands.

Chapter 4 also noted that Presbyterians don't have clergy persons (although people speak of them). Officers for Presbyterians include presbyters and deacons.[2] A characteristic of ministry in the Presbyterian Church (U.S.A.) is mutuality of service or parity of officers. In a church session, the pastor is always outnumbered by the elders. In the other governing bodies, the number of Ministers of Word and Sacrament and elders is at least equal. In every respect, each officer gets one vote.

All officers are considered to be called to their position by God through the voice of the people. The Presbyterian understanding of call is that it comes in three parts. First, there is an inner or personal call, a desire to serve Jesus Christ through the church. The second aspect is a recognition by a group of God's people that the individual indeed has appropriate gifts and skills for service. Finally, there is the vote by a governing body confirming the validity of the call. Without the second and third aspects, there is only a personal sense of being called. A call requires validation by the community.

When one is ordained as an elder or as a Minister of Word and Sacrament, the person is an officer of the Presbyterian Church (U.S.A.). Service is in a specific place for a specific purpose. Membership in a governing body is never automatic when one moves from one form of ministry to another. Ordination is to function and is not understood to alter the person. Once ordained, a person may lose the office only by renouncing the jurisdiction of the church, by being found guilty in a disciplinary case, by laying the office aside, or by dying.

Ordination involves taking nine vows, beginning with a reaffirmation of the vows of church membership. Other vows concern matters of belief and order. These vows highlight the affirmation that Jesus Christ is Head of the church and summarize the obligations of officers to Jesus Christ and to the church. Service as an officer is an opportunity to practice discipleship as a servant-disciple. The vows are challenging (if not overwhelming) when considered together. An officer who acts contrary to the obligations outlined in the vows is liable to church discipline.

As pointed out in chapter 5, Presbyterian commitment to the proposition that "theology matters"[3] means that the tensions between faith, truth, and mission frequently emerge in our fellowship. Our faith is in the sovereign God whom we know most thoroughly through God's Son, Jesus Christ. By the gift of the Holy Spirit, we also have Scriptures that are a written testimony to God and God's acts. Faith is what emerges when we discover God's forgiveness, together with all the other blessings God gives us.

Truth, according to Jesus, bears good fruit. This may sound like philosophical pragmatism, yet the fruit metaphor suggests that the time factor is significant. Jesus' teaching also points toward the importance of "doing the truth."[4] While thinking about the faith (which is theology) is important, the final test is the sort of fruit that comes of it.

Fruit, in Jesus' metaphor, provides the basis for what today we understand as the mission of the church: an inclusive enterprise in which all believers participate in according to the gifts God has given them. The mission of the Presbyterian Church (U.S.A.) is breathtaking in its scope and exceeds what is familiar to many. The fruits of mission are not always immediately apparent, which disturbs those committed to immediate results. According to Jesus, it is not a question of how soon the fruit comes, but whether it abides.[5] The ultimate fruit of mission is the coming of God's realm, the timing of which is out of human hands.[6]

The tensions identified in chapter 5 enable us to understand why and how dialogues about theology and mission become so intense. We need to keep in mind that how we go about discussing and debating issues such as these is as much a matter of faithfulness as the issues themselves.

Diversity of perspectives emerge when we discuss faith and mission, so chapter 6 explored diversity in the Presbyterian Church (U.S.A.). Our faith declares that "in Christ God was reconciling the world to himself,"[7] and in so doing identifies a ministry given to us. As we mature in faith, we engage in the enterprise of "working out [our] own salvation with fear and trembling,"[8] which is how our faith becomes part of us. Our faith in the incarnation of God in Jesus Christ is paralleled by a belief that believers incarnate God's grace in various ways. Diversity is a necessary and inescapable outcome. Each particular Presbyterian church has distinctive features arising from the pastors, the people, their history, and their location. The same is true of presbytery meetings. What is surprising is how often people are dismayed by diversity. The New Testament demonstrates diversity in many ways, not least of which are the four Gospels, which have diverse ways of telling the story of our faith's beginning. Diversity is inherent in our concern about outreach through mission. Diversity also poses the question, "Have we gone beyond some sort of limit?" As the early church struggled with whether non-Hebrews should be considered Christians, so we continue to increase our diversity while seeking to maintain "the unity of the Spirit in the bond of peace" (Eph. 4:3).

Chapter 7 focused on the tensions inherent in a representative democracy. By its nature, this form of government works to the degree that people understand how authority is distributed within the group. The people in a particular church elect officers by majority vote. Those elected and ordained assume certain responsibilities regarding life in that church. Members of the congregation have fewer, but equally explicit responsibilities.

Presbyterian officers work together in groups. Elders work with the pastor on the session, which has explicit and extensive responsibilities. No single officer may make a decision regarding any of these responsibilities; rather, the rule is that a majority shall decide. The only indispensable member of the session is the moderator, a Minister of Word and Sacrament, and usually the pastor, without whom there cannot be a session meeting (except in extraordinary circumstances). This approach requires mutuality in determining the direction of the church's life and mission. This mutuality also lies behind the need for committees. Officers may be selected to serve as commissioners in other governing bodies, in which there is always a balance of elders and Ministers of Word and Sacrament. The presbytery is the only governing body with the authority to assume responsibilities other than those delineated, and they do so only when those responsibilities are not otherwise assigned.

The basis for this emphasis on decisions made in groups is biblical and theological. The so-called Council of Jerusalem is foundational for this understanding of church decision making (Acts 15). The theological assumption is that God's Spirit is at work when dedicated persons engage in discussion and struggle with the decisions.

Chapter 8 introduced the tension between power and authority. In Presbyterian polity, power is considered a gift that Jesus Christ gives to the church for the purpose of mission. Power used otherwise is an abuse of power. As indicated earlier, the *Book of Order* explicitly assigns authority to groups by indicating areas for which the group is responsible.

Chapter 9 addressed the topic of church discipline. The eighth Historic Principle reminds us that a concern for "decency and order" requires provision for when trouble arises. "Problems" provide the challenge to put our commitment to our Savior into action and becomes an opportunity for redemptive action. The tension inherent in such situations lies between the health and integrity of the church on the one hand, and the spiritual health of the person(s) involved on the other. The goal is healing.

As we go about the business of discipline, we continue to be witnesses for our professed faith. The effectiveness of church life requires an internal integrity of faith and practice. The internal life of the church is not insulated from those outside the community of faith. Thus, how we go about all of our church work, especially our discipline, has the potential to enhance or undercut our witness to those beyond our fellowship. The procedural detail found in the "Rules of Discipline" may seem intimidating or unnecessary until we consider the delicacy of the tensions involved. Chapter 1 of the "Rules of Discipline" provides an eloquent reminder of how we are to be a "provisional demonstration of the Kingdom of God,"[9] especially when we enter this challenging, often neglected area of church life.

Beyond those present within the Historic Principles, there are tensions between the principles. It is important to recognize that tensions were an intended (or at least accepted) aspect within the *Book of Order* from its inception.[10] The question for us is to determine what function such tensions within the document might serve. Why were these principles put together as they are? This is not to suppose that we can discover at this late date what was the original intent of that committee, any more than we can establish with certainly what those who wrote the Constitution of the United States of America intended in certain clauses.[11] But we can consider the possibilities.

I propose as an hypothesis that the drafters were more pastor-theologians than political scientists. Their pastoral experience, together with their theological and confessional knowledge, had given them some wisdom regarding life in the church.[12] A political, structural, or legal approach to understanding the principles without careful consideration of the pastoral and theological dimension risks losing some of the wisdom of our heritage. I, therefore, propose that we consider the tensions identified in this volume as caution signs in church life. The principles have endured for two centuries, providing ongoing guidance and counsel to Presbyterians. There is more guidance yet to be gained from the principles.

There is also a tension between the *Book of Order* and *Book of Confessions*. There appears to be a tendency to evaluate provisions of the *Book of Order* with criteria that does not include the rest of the Constitution. Biblical and theological assessments have been made without reference to the *Book of Confessions*. This study has demonstrated that the *Book of Confessions* provides a helpful link, revealing connections between Scripture and the present *Book of Order*. Such a constitutional approach enables us to appreciate the richness of our polity.

In fact, the Constitution of the Presbyterian Church (U.S.A.) depicts a way of being Presbyterian that offers considerable guidance in a time when many seek it. There is evidenced within it a high value on disciples caring for one another amid the ambiguities and tensions of church life. When the *Book of Order* gets precise and prescriptive, it is highlighting an area that has, in the past, been found perilous for people of faith. It reminds us that the church belongs to God. This reminder can be challenging and make us uncomfortable. The *Book of Order* is best approached as a guide for Presbyterian disciples as they mature in faith.

At times as a seminary polity teacher approaching a new class, I have wondered whether the polity I was teaching would survive the period of my students' ministries. We will be faced with periodic challenges to the continuing wholeness of the Presbyterian Church (U.S.A.). On the threshold of the twenty-first century, Presbyterians are approaching a time when our call to mission will be experienced as more demanding, more extensive, and more diverse than in the past. Faithfulness as part of Christ's church requires trusting one another as we go about God's business. It also requires remembering that we are all loved by God in Christ, and by that love, we are compelled to love one another, as Christ has loved us.

otes

1. Adapted from Eph. 4:1.

2. There are also trustees to handle corporate relations between churches and civil authority. Trustees are not ordained to their office.

3. "Report of the Assembly Committee on General Assembly Council Review," in *Minutes of the 206th General Assembly* (1994), p. 87.

4. "Those who do what is true come to the light" (John 3:21). Note 1 John 1:6 where those who are not doing the truth are said to be in darkness. See also G-1.0304.

5. See John 15:16.

6. See Matt. 24:36 and Mark 13:32.

7. 1 Cor. 5:19. This verse provides the theme of the Confession of 1967 (*Book of Confessions*, 9.07).

8. Phil. 2:12. See Kathleen Norris, *Amazing Grace* (New York: Riverhead Books, 1998), pp. 37–44, where she meditates on conversion.

9. See G-3.0200.

10. The wording of the principles suggests that the drafters recognized that some would perceive tensions between some principles. Some clues to this are the initial clauses of G-1.0302; 1.0305; 1.0306.

11. For example, see Leonard W. Levy, *Original Intent and the Framer's Constitution* (New York: Macmillan Publishing Company, 1988).

12. The important paper, "Historic Principles, Conscience, and Church Government" (Louisville: Office of the General Assembly, 1983), p. 3, which is available from Presbyterian Distribution Services (OGA-88-059), provides sketches of the drafters that provide initial support for this hypothesis.

$\mathcal{S}$uggestions for Leaders

$\mathcal{T}$his book offers a different approach to Presbyterian polity, in the hope that the process of "making sense" of how we go about being a church will be clearer to persons new to responsibility as officers, as well as to those experienced officers who have not had the opportunity to study the *Book of Order*. Teaching based on *History and Theology in the Book of Order* will depend on several factors. Primarily, the leader will use experience and knowledge in dialogue with the text. This study guide provides clues and resources from which the leader may choose. It offers a series of suggestions for organizing the material in appropriate ways for the given audience. Other factors include where the sessions are held, the number of sessions, the length of each session, the number of participants, what resources are available, and what equipment is available (physically present and also comfortable for you to use). The teacher's own style of presenting material is an essential ingredient to the process. Since the word *mutual* appears nineteen times in the *Book of Order*, it is important that there be give and take for learning to occur. This is especially true with adults.

The assumption is that every participant for officer training will have a copy of the *Book of Order* and the *Book of Confessions* (G-14.0205). The training is assigned to provide an introduction to these two resources so that officers will grow in appreciation of how Presbyterian polity works in the interests of mission. Implicit in all this is my awareness that polity has to do with putting into practice our understanding of the Presbyterian Church (U.S.A.) as a part of the body of Christ. The *Book of Order* may fruitfully be approached as an instrument for caring for the body of Christ, where civility and respect govern the way we work together as disciples of our Lord and Savior, Jesus Christ.

As people enter into a study of polity, they might well consider Gen. 32:22–33 as a description of the experience ahead of them. The *Book of Order* is not as easy to understand as it may appear to be. There is intricate interconnection within its covers, as well as myriad interconnections with Scripture and the *Book of Confessions*. To be governed by our church's polity and to abide by its discipline is not an easy task. However, we, as officers, commit ourselves to the endeavor.

Step 1. Introducing the Study

1. Begin with an introduction exercise so that those gathered can settle in for their work together as growing officers of the Presbyterian Church (U.S.A.) and of their local congregations.

2. Consider with the group the progression of vows (G-14.0207).

   - What is the first vow?

   - Why do you think that comes first?

   - What does that suggest about serving as an officer?

- How do questions 2, 3, and 5 combine with each other? (These three suggest that Scripture and confessions are basic to polity, the approach this study adopts.)
- What is the relationship between questions 1–4 and the remaining questions? (Have the group propose how the remaining questions flow from the first four. The flow may be understood as follows (see figure 1):

source of faith

authoritative written witness to faith

basic articulation of Reformed faith

personal commitment to learn from 2 and 3

polity as operational implications of 2 and 3

commitment to implement mission in a spirit of love

concern for the health of the body of Christ

commitment to four cardinal virtues of office

agreement to serve in a specific role

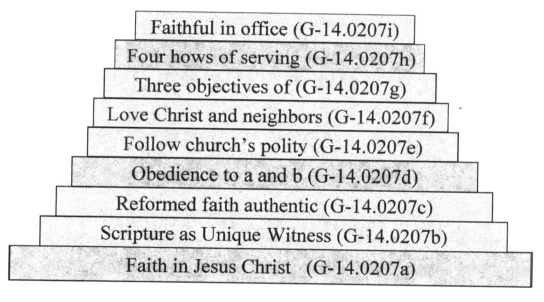

Faithful in office (G-14.0207i)

Four hows of serving (G-14.0207h)

Three objectives of (G-14.0207g)

Love Christ and neighbors (G-14.0207f)

Follow church's polity (G-14.0207e)

Obedience to a and b (G-14.0207d)

Reformed faith authentic (G-14.0207c)

Scripture as Unique Witness (G-14.0207b)

Faith in Jesus Christ (G-14.0207a)

FIGURE 1. BUILDING LAYERS OF PRESBYTERIAN UNDERSTANDING

3. Another task for this session is to introduce the class to the *Book of Order* and the *Book of Confessions*, guided by material in chapter 1 of this book. Discuss the similarities and differences in the reference systems of the two books.

4. Have participants turn in their copies to G-14.0205 in the *Book of Order*. Ask someone to read the paragraph. Explain that the study will provide them with the basic knowledge for serving as officers.

5. Ask the participants for their concerns about the study. Write these down on newsprint so that these concerns may be addressed during the study.

6. Indicate to the participants that they should bring their Bibles, *Book of Order*, and *Book of Confessions* to each training session, since they will be using all three. This also prepares them for bringing the *Book of Order* with them to meetings. ("Never leave home without it.")

7. Assign material to prepare for the next session:

   a. Read G-1.0000 in the *Book of Order*.

   b. Suggest that they consider the meaning of the sequence of the five sections.

Step 2: Basic Orientation

Note: This step in the process is critical for enabling officers to use the *Book of Order* as a resource for ministry. This session introduces both the way the *Book of Order* is presented as well as an analysis of the first chapter.

1. Explore some various understandings of the concept of *order.*

2. Supervise practice using the *Book of Order*. Drill the class in finding references. You may choose your own or use the following references. Expect some problems and patiently help the group members gain confidence using this necessary skill. (The references could be on flash cards or written on newsprint or chalkboard.) Have the one who finds the reference read it out loud. Some suggestions are as follows:

   a. G-2.0100

   b. G-10.0210

   c. G-18.0301

   d. W-1.4004

   e. D-1.0102

   f. G-9.0409a(2)

   g. G-1.0502j(2)

   h. W-6.2002

3. Ask whether there are questions regarding the numbering system. Note that there are *no* page numbers for the *Book of Order*, yet the *Book of Confessions* has them.

4. Read each paragraph out loud slowly. Before going to the next paragraph, identify the focus of the paragraph. Note any "surprises."

5. Have the group turn together to G-1.0000. Point out the four paragraphs of G-1.0100. Have the group divide into teams or do the following together.

   a. Develop a brief (5–10 word) summary of the paragraph.

   b. Go to the next paragraph, repeat steps a–c until finished.

   c. Discuss how this sequence of paragraphs presents an understanding of why and how life in the church is organized.

    d. Have the groups report their findings regarding D-1.0102. Also, list the "surprises" that emerged in these four paragraphs.

    e. Summarize the theological progression of this section.

       Christ is Lord of all power.

       Christ created the Church, gave it his power.

       Appropriate uses of Christ's power given to the Church.

       How we are to live thankfully for Christ's power.

6. Turn to G-2.0100a and have the group read it. Mention that the image of the body of Christ is suggested in G-1.0100 and will continue to be present throughout the *Book of Order*.

7. Clarify the meaning of the word *ends* used here. One synonym is "purposes."

8. Ask if any have seen the "Great Ends of the Church" before. (Moderator John Buchanan of the 208th General Assembly (1996) made these Great Ends a major focus for our church.)

   - Discuss how these "Great Ends" might be used in the life of the church.

   - Offer as final comments a summary of the discussion of "Principles" at the end of chapter 1 of "History and Theology" in the *Book of Order*. This provides the final piece of the foundation for the training. Suggest that participants read through the material related the next step before the next session.

Step 3. Conscience and Community

1. Begin this session by introducing the concept of "tension." The thesis is that the Historic Principles identify tensions within the life of the church. These tensions serve to alert us to issues in church life that must be addressed with care.

2. Depending on the interests and orientation of the group, you might use one of the following options (or combine them):

Conceptual

- Using the epigraph, initiate a discussion on conscience as an aspect of human personality.

- Discuss the title of C. Ellis Nelson's book, *Don't Let Your Conscience Be Your Guide*.

- Contrast positive and negative conscience, using *Book of Confessions*, 6.100.

- Read and discuss Gal. 2:1–10 and 1 Cor. 10:23–25.

- Examine the first Historic Principle together, in the light of the confessional sources so that the group may consider how this modifies their understanding of conscience.

Theological

- Read and discuss Gal. 2:1–10, 1 Cor. 10:23–25, and Acts 15, considering the context.

- Examine the first Historic Principle, in the light of the confessional sources so that the group may consider how this modifies their understanding of conscience.

- Consider G-6.0106a and G-6.0106b and its implications, along with G-9.0303 to G-9.0305, as well as G-6.0500. How do these provisions demonstrate the principle in action?

3. Figure 2 attempts to show relationships related to conscience and community. Use it as you see fit (overhead, photocopy, etc.).

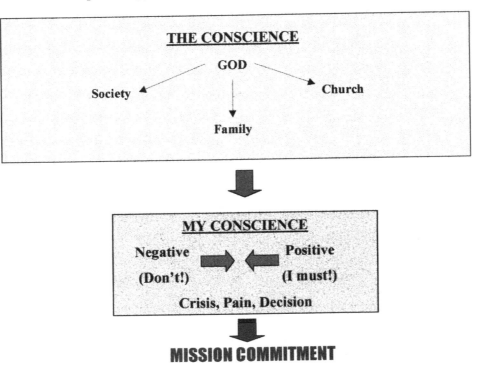

FIGURE 2. CONSCIENCE FOR PRESBYTERIANS

4. It is critically important to clarify the following points in this session:

   a. The key word in the first Historic Principle is *conscience*.

   b. *Conscience* is the intensely personal way values are integrated into our lives. It is a combination of family influences, community interaction, church teachings, and one's experience of God.

   c. *Conscience* includes both positive and negative aspects. The conscience transformed by God's grace thus provides energy for mission.

   d. *Conscience* is never sovereign since we believe that God is Lord of all, including the conscience.

e. Presbyterians take conscience very seriously, as indicated by the provisions for allowing persons to leave the fellowship when conscience moves them, with only minor notice.

f. Officers in the Presbyterian system agree that issues of conscience are deeply personal, but also require the counsel of colleagues in ministry.

5. Make the assignment for the next session.

Step 4. Decisions at the Boundaries

Note: Leader may wish to jump ahead to step 5, then come back to this one.

1. Begin by asking the group for their understandings of Jesus as the Good Shepherd.

   a. Record initial comments.

   b. Read Matt. 18:10–14 and discuss the passage.

   c. Turn to John 10:1–18 (perhaps choosing which verses are appropriate).

   d. Compare the two presentations, exploring what the difference is, how it affects our understanding of Christ as Good Shepherd.

   e. Ask if the church has a gatekeeping function.

2. Turn to Acts 15:1 and divide into groups or read the passage together.

   a. Have the group discuss how the so-called Council of Jerusalem handled their crisis over criteria for membership in the church.

   b. How did they distribute their resolution of the controversy?

   c. Why were the conditions of membership necessary?

   d. How would the church's development have been different without this decision?

3. Display figure 3 (p. 112), in order to discuss the necessity for social boundaries.

   a. Have the group relate any experiences in crossing political borders, describing what they felt.

   b. Inquire about their feelings when they got their first driver's license.

   c. Suggest that these are social borders that must be crossed in the course of life. Discuss figure 3 (p. 112), indicating circles of involvement in the church.

   • The outer circle (Circle of Fellowship) is shown with a dotted line to indicate that this is a porous boundary, where people may enter and leave at will.

   • The inner circle (Circle of Membership) has a definite boundary across which persons must enter and leave in specific ways.

   • The innermost circle (Circle of Responsibility) also has a definite boundary together with specific ways of entering and leaving.

4. Turn to the second Historic Principle (G-1.0302) and have the group read it.

   a. Note how the boundaries are expressed in the principle. *Note*: There is also the boundary between churches, not included in figure 3.

b. Clarify any words or phrases that the participants do not understand.

c. Discuss the potentially volatile comment about responsibility ("too lax or too narrow") and its effect on the liberty or rights of others.

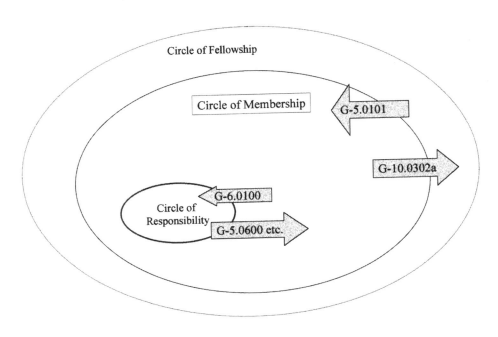

FIGURE 3. CHURCH BORDER CROSSINGS

5. Examine some confessional material relevant to this discussion.

   a. Second Helvetic Confession, 5.139–140, pp. 90–91.

   b. Westminster Confession, 6.140, 6.141, 6.143, and 6.144, pp. 156–157.

6. Consider the Circle of Fellowship in the *Book of Order*.

   a. Examine G-5.0300 for the status of nonmembers.

   b. Compare G-5.0301c with W-2.3012a–e.

7. Consider the Circle of Membership in the *Book of Order*.

   a. Note G-5.0401 for who is responsible for preparation.

   b. Review G-5.0100 for the four entrances into the membership circle and the meaning of membership.

   c. Examine G-7.0103 and G-7.0201 and discuss their pertinence for all members.

   d. Review G-5.0102 regarding responsibilities of membership.

   e. Note G-5.0501 regarding responsibility for review of membership.

   f. Summarize exits from membership indicated in G-10.0302a(2)(c)–b(8).

8. Consider the Circle of Responsibility.

   a. Identify the understanding of ordination for function shown in G-6.0100, particularly G-6.0105 and G-6.0106, which is entrance into the Circle of Responsibility.

   b. Point out how the three-step ordination process works for both presbyters and deacons with specific reference to G-14.0205.

   c. Review the role of officers (G-6.0104) and the specific responsibilities in G-6.0300 for elders and G-6.0700 for deacons.

   d. Turn to G-4.0301, "Principles of Presbyterian Government," and discuss how these affect the work of officers.

   e. Exits from the Circle of Responsibility are as follows:

      • resignation and release from exercise (G-14.0210–0211).

      • renunciation of jurisdiction (G-6.0500)

      • judicial process will be covered later in Step 9. Provide a case from your experience (or the one included in the Ordinands' booklet) demonstrating that the entrances and exits each involve the need to discern what to do, in the sense of G-4.0301d: "Presbyters are not simply to reflect the will of the people, but rather to seek together to find and represent the will of Christ."

9. Opportunity for questions, comments, assignment for the next session.

Step 5. Church Officers

1. Begin by asking the officers their understandings of "priesthood of all believers."

   a. Have them turn to 5.153 in the *Book of Confessions*. Note the distinction between "priesthood" and "ministry."

   b. Look at the Second Helvetic Confession (5.155), regarding ministers.

   c. Note that this chapter of continues with a description of various aspects of ministry.

2. Explore the implications of the third Historic Principle (G-1.0303).

   a. Read it through together.

   b. Use grammatical analysis to help clarify the structure of the passage.

   c. Note that the second section points out the possibilities for error, as well as the understandings of the implications of those errors.

3. Examine some references in the *Book of Order* related to ministry.

   a. Read together G-1.0303.

   b. Consider what seems surprising to the group and discuss these surprises.

   c. Note section 3.18 in the *Book of Confessions*, where the "marks of the church" are presented. (You may want to highlight these.)

   d. Which of these aspects of the work of officers does the group find challenging? Discuss these, indicating that they will have opportunity to explore this in more detail later.

e. Remind the group of the importance of keeping in mind the Pauline metaphor of the church as the body of Christ.

4. Consider the purpose of the church—*mission*.

   a. Turn to G-3.0100.

   b. Invite the group to read through this section, noting surprises.

   c. Discuss the surprises.

5. Which officers?

   a. Read together G-6.0102–0103.

   b. Look at *Book of Confessions*, 5.150, regarding how ministers are to be chosen.

   c. Look at 1 Tim. 3:1–7 (where "overseer" and "presbyter" are both used) as well as 3:8–13 regarding deacons. Consider Titus 1:5–9 where "elder" and "bishop" appears to be used interchangeably.

   d. Move back to G-6.0106 for the paragraph regarding lifestyle.

   e. Point out the limits to conscience indicated for officers in G-6.0108b.

   f. Turn to G-10.0101, which is one of many references to the need for mutuality in governing bodies for the Presbyterian system to work efficiently. You may, if there is time, also refer to W-1.4004–4006 as another instance of mutuality.

6. Turn to the final criterion of the principle: "observing in all cases, the rules contained in the Word of God."

   a. Note that this undergirds the affirmation of G-2.0200.

   b. Point out that there is also an implicit principle in G-2.0000 that Scripture needs to be examined through the lens of the *Book of Confessions*, as is demonstrated in this study.

7. Include time for questions and clarify the assignment for the next session.

Step 6. Faith, Truth, and Mission

1. Begin with a Bible study of Matt. 7:15–20.

   a. Read the full paragraph. Compare with Luke 6:43–45. Look also at Deut. 18:21–22 as an earlier way of expressing this point.

   b. What seems to be the focus of Jesus' teaching?

   c. Why are false prophets so difficult to detect?

   d. What is the test by which truth is determined according to this teaching?

   e. According to Luke, what is the root of the difference between good and bad?

2. Have the group consider, then discuss, their understanding of one or more of the following references in the *Book of Confessions*.

   a. C-7.077 and C-7.078 (Note the connection of "require" and "forbidden.")

   b. C-6.075–076 (Note the progression here.)

c. C-9.22–23 (This establishes a continuity with the previous two.)

3. Read through G-1.0304 together using the *Book of Order* and attending to grammatical analysis. Encourage participants to voice their questions about this principle.

4. Examine some or all of these references to the *Book of Order*. (Those with an asterisk [*] are particularly important.)

   a. *G-1.0100b, first sentence

   b. *G-2.0100b, first sentence

   c. *G-3.0200c

   d. G-5.0102

   e. *G-10.0102, introduction

   f. G-14.0103

5. Initiate a discussion about the interrelationship between truth and mission.

   a. What is appropriate "fruit" that flows from the perspective that truth and mission are on the same level?

   b. Look at 1 Cor. 14:7–12 and note the context.

   c. Reflect on how this enriches the understanding of the Lordship of Jesus Christ, the head of the body of Christ, the church.

6. Look again at the ordination questions for elders (G-14.0207) and discuss whether they are presented in a sequence consistent with this principle.

7. Make the assignment for the next session.

Step 7. Differences and Diversity

1. Discuss the meaning of the word *forbearance* (if any) to the participants.

   a. Have a dictionary definition available, possibly in a handout. Describe forbearance as an old word for showing mercy.

   b. Study Jesus' parable in Matt. 18:21–35. Discuss the lack of mercy in this parable, and what showing mercy would be in the parable.

2. Have someone read the Sixth Commandment (Ex. 20:13).

   a. Look up duties required in the Sixth Commandment as described in the Larger Catechism (*Book of Confessions*, 7.245).

   b. What does the inclusion of forbearance in this list suggest?

3. Turn to G-4.0400.

   a. Assist the group in distinguishing between diversity and inclusiveness.

   b. Invite the participants to consider in terms of how diverse their local church is the categories of diversity in G-4.0403.

c. Have some indication of the backgrounds of those present, indicating the diversity present in the group (such as previous home community, type of work experience, etc.). Review the data in chapter 6 of this book regarding the diversity of the PC(USA).

4. Reflect on how Presbyterians seek to honor the commitments to diversity. The following provisions are relevant to this discussion.

   a. G-14.0201b

   b. G-5.0103

   c. G-10.0301, second sentence

   d. G-9.0104–0106

   e. The "Resolution on Racial Ethnic New Church Development and Redevelopment" to the 208th General Assembly (1996), especially 33.148, p. 378.

5. Refer to the second major clause of G-1.0305, noting specifically one or more of the following:

   Matt. 7:12

   John 17:21

   1 John 3:14, 16

   1 Cor. 1:11

   1 Cor. 12:27

   1 Peter 3:8–9

   G-4.0201d

6. Suggest a conversation on the tension between forbearance and advocacy.

7. Make the assignment for the next session.

Step 8. Who Chooses Whom and Why?

1. Describe and discuss the three types of church polity (Congregational, Episcopal, Presbyterian), using the group's experience as much as possible.

2. Clarify the terminology for officers (presbyters, Ministers of the Word and Sacrament, elders, deacons) in the Presbyterian system.
   Note: There is no clergy/laity distinction for Presbyterians.

3. Explore with the participants the scriptural foundation for these offices.

4. Clarify the significance of enumerated powers. (This will be developed more fully in the next step.)

   a. Note the role of the congregation in G-7.0304.

   b. Review how a pastor is called to ministry.

   c. Review the process for nominating committee of the congregation.

   d. Revisit the three-part understanding of call.

5. Stress the importance of the people calling their own officers. Note that it is an inalienable right, with certain limits.

6. Conclude with an emphasis on the corporate decisions of session (not board of elders).

7. Make assignments for the next session.

Step 9. Power versus Authority

1. Differentiate between power and authority.

   a. Ask how the group would define *power* in terms of human relationships.

   b. How does the word *authority* differ from "power"? Ask participants to give an illustration of appropriate and inappropriate exercises of power.

2. Turn to the seventh Historic Principle and highlight the phrase "church power."

   a. How does the discussion thus far illuminate the phrase?

   b. Where does the church's power come from? (Reference to G-1.0100a may focus the discussion.)

   • What are the proper uses of that power? (Reference to G-1.0100b may focus the discussion.)

   • How does the phrase "ministerial and declarative" affect an understanding of the use of church power?

   • Explore meanings for the term *declarative* as it might relate to the process of Christian witness. (Resources relevant to this are found in W-6.1001, W-6.1002, W-6.3001, W-6.3002, W-6.3011.)

3. Have half the group read John 13:1–9, and the other read Matt. 20:24–28. What do these readings suggest about the exercise of power by disciples?

   a. How do these two passages affect your understanding of the purpose of church power?

   b. Discuss the Second Helvetic Confession's statements on church power (*Book of Confessions*, 5.157, 5.159, 5.160).

4. Review the general powers of governing bodies in 9.0102b. Note how G-9.0103 stresses "mutual relations."

5. Discuss the nineteen *responsibilities* of session in G-10.0102. Note how the word *responsibilities* affects the understanding of service in ministry. Divide the group into smaller discussion groups, if possible, to explore the these questions.

   a. Which of these responsibilities surprised you and how?

   b. Which of these responsibilities do you think we are not implementing as a church?

   c. Which one of these responsibilities should challenge us as a session in the coming year?

   d. Which of these responsibilities speaks to you personally as a call or challenge to your talents and interests?

6. Make appropriate assignments for the next session.

Step 10. Decency, Order, and Discipline

1. Begin with a discussion of 1 Cor. 14:40.

   a. Suggest that this is an often-repeated phrase in Presbyterian circles.

   b. Summarize the context of 1 Corinthians 14. (The issue is the use of "spiritual gifts" without regard for newcomers.)

   c. Note that 1 Cor. 14:40 follows a semicolon, so it is only part of a sentence.

   d. Allow the group to discuss what they see as the importance of order for life in a community of faith.

2. Discuss the word *disciple*.

   a. Ask the group how they understand the word *disciple*.

   b. Read Matt. 10:1–4, where Jesus calls disciples, and verses 24–25, which are the basic ground rules for discipleship. Discuss what this suggests about Jesus' expectations of one who is his disciple.

3. Explore what understandings and feelings participants have about the word *discipline*.

   a. Discuss meanings of "discipline" as the participants understand it. (Expect both negative and positive associations. Write down all suggestions.)

   b. Read *Book of Confessions*, 4.083 and 4.085.

   • Peter is usually understood as having the "power of the keys" (Matt. 16:17–19). How does the Heidelberg Catechism interpret this?

   • Discuss the participants' response to this interpretation of the Matthew passage.

4. Discuss the phrase from G-1.0307: "the vigor and strictness of its discipline. . . ."

   a. How does this reflect the positive and negative aspects of discipline?

   b. Recall from the first Historic Principle the two aspects of conscience and explore how those two competing aspects may be present in the concept of discipline.

   c. Discuss how commitment to the good news affects response to departures from "good order."

5. Discuss briefly the two types of cases identified in D-2.0202.

   a. Remedial: irregularity and delinquency

   b. Disciplinary: involving one or more offenses

6. Review G-1.0308. Considering sharing with the group a recent decision of the General Assembly Permanent Judicial Commission to illustrate how matters of discipline are handled.

7. Make assignments for the next session.

Step 11. Connecting Presbyterians

1. Introduce the phrase "connectional church."

    a. Ask what connections the group members see in the Presbyterian Church (U.S.A.).

    b. Discuss the importance of such connections.

    c. Introduce G-1.0400 and note that it was adopted in 1797 as a statement regarding central unifying factors.

2. Discuss the first part of G-1.0400

    a. Note the importance placed on the local congregations in G-7.0102.

    b. Refer to the Second Helvetic Confession's position in this matter (*Book of Confessions*, 5.126, 5.127, and 5.128)

3. Discuss the role of ascending governing bodies as described in clauses 2 and 3 of G-1.0400.

    a. Review the concept of representative democracy (chapter 7 of this book).

    b. Differentiate between the Presbyterian connectional and the Congregational system of autonomous congregations.

    c. Relate the connectional system to Rom. 12:5 as a way of witnessing to the body of Christ.

    d. Explain how a *commissioner* (given the responsibility of voting on behalf of the one who has commissioned him or her) differs from a *representative* (expected to re-present the views of the electorate). See G-4.0301d.

4. Note exceptions to clause 4, which articulates that a majority shall govern.

    a. Amending the *Book of Confessions* G-18.0201a(2), and election of a pastor (G-14.0505).

    b. Discuss the reasons for such limits, which are protection of the rights of the minority and protection for the document on which the system is based (similar to amending the Constitution of the United States of America).

5. Discuss appeals in clause 5.

    a. Note that this process relies on ascending governing bodies.

    b. Note that the concern for fair treatment requires increasingly broader perspectives in the resolution of disputes.

6. Conclude by discussing figure 1. Note how the nine questions expand on the vows of membership.

Evaluation

The following are some suggestions for complying with G-14.0205.

1. Have each candidate choose a tension from the study, explore how that tension might arise in a session, and how the *Book of Order* and the *Book of Confessions* provide guidance for such situations.

2. Have each candidate provide three citations from the Constitution relating to Carolyn Winfrey Gilette's hymn, "Our God, We Are a Church Reformed,"[1] or assign a stanza to each candidate. After the report, the session could sing the hymn together, or even use it when the candidates are ordained. Here are some suggested connections.

Hymn Text	References
Our God, we are a church reformed, A church reforming still; We long to grow in your true Word, And follow more your will.	G-2.0200, last sentence *Book of Confessions*, 7.277
How awesome is your sovereign rule; You reign from heav'n above, Yet you knelt down in Jesus Christ, In sacrifice and love.	G-2.0500a *Book of Confessions*, 9.08 and 9.40 Phil. 2:6–11; *Book of Confessions*, 6.044–046
In love, you bring your people here And call your church to you, That we may know salvation's joy And serve in all we do.	G-2.0100b; 3.0000; 5.0102
In love, you draw your people here And call your church to you, That we may know salvation's joy And serve in all we do.	G-1.0100b; 3.0300a, b G-7.001, 7.0711 G-2.0100b; 3.0000; 5.0102
You call us to community; By faith our hearts are stirred. In church, we seek an ordered life, According to your Word.	G-1.0100b, c; 4.0101 G-1.0300; *Book of Confessions*, 9.34 G-1.0100c
As faithful stewards we find joy; We need no rich display. Lord, teach us all to use with care The gifts you give each day.	G-2.0500a(3); W-2.5003 G-1.0100c; 5.0102d; W-7.5003
The world makes gods of lesser things, and wrongly uses power; So by your Spirit may we work For justice every hour.	G-2.0500a(4) *Book of Confessions*, 9.53 G-3.0300c(3)

3. Assign a sentence or two from the *Book of Order* to the participants, asking them to write a brief essay for the church newsletter. Ask them to consider how the statement may surprise some Presbyterians, and also how it speaks directly to what it means to be Presbyterian. Some suggestions for sentences are as follows:

G-1.0100b	G-3.0200b	G-4.0301h	G-8.0201
G-1.0100c	G-3.0200c	G-4.0302	G-9.0401
G-2.0100b	G-3.0400	G-4.0303	G-9.0403
G-2.0500b	G-4.0104	G-4.0401	G-10.0102
G-3.0200	G-4.0201	G-5.0501	G-14.0103
G-3.0200a	G-4.0301d	G-7.0103	D-1.0101

4. Play Devil's Advocate, a game that raises issues for discussion. Ask participants to respond to each challenge, referring to the *Book of Order*.[2]

"It doesn't matter that the pastor is out of town. Any one of the elders could baptize your baby."

Response: Are elders *authorized* to baptize?

"You're the teacher. Go ahead and use whatever materials you like."

Response: Who is *responsible* for the content of teaching in the church school?

"You know more about music than anyone else in the congregation. Choose the hymns and special music you think are best."

Response: Who is *authorized* to choose the music for worship?

"Since you have to clean up this place, you should decide who can use the building and when."

Response: Who is *accountable* for the use of church property?

"Since you're the head of the church, you should decide who may or may not join the church."

Response: Who is *authorized* to receive and dismiss members? Who has this power?

"If you don't like how the pastor preaches, do something about it. Choose the passages from the Bible you like. Tell the pastor what should be preached from *your* pulpit?"

Response: Who is *authorized* by the *Book of Order* to choose Bible passages for worship?

Q. Who determines what constitutes acceptable interpretation?

5. Adapt a question from the Ordination Exams for candidates for ministry of Word and Sacrament. The following is one suggested adaptation.

A member approaches you as an elder in active service after church, and says:

The paper this morning reports the action of the General Assembly on gun control. They sure weren't representing my position. Who elected those people? Why do they make such outrageous statements? What right do they have to express their opinions?

Respond to each of the four questions raised by the member, with reference to the *Book of Order*.

Note: You might photocopy Commissioners' Resolution 98–19, which was the basis for the action. The text is found in the *Minutes of the 210th General Assembly* (1998), p. 746. The action of the General Assembly is reported on p. 57.

 Notes

1. Carolyn Winfrey Gilette, "Our God, We Are a Church," in *The Presbyterian Outlook* (October 26, 1988), p. 2. Used by permission.

2. This is adapted from a training program developed by Rev. Isaac Butterworth, First Presbyterian Church, Wichita Falls, Texas. Used with permission. (Italics indicate clues to an accurate response.)

*I*ndex of Subjects

Book of Order

Form of Government

Directory for Worship

Rules of Discipline

Book of Confessions

Scripture

$\mathcal{I}$ndex of General Assembly Documents

*Reprinted in 1983

Index of Authors